THE BRIDE

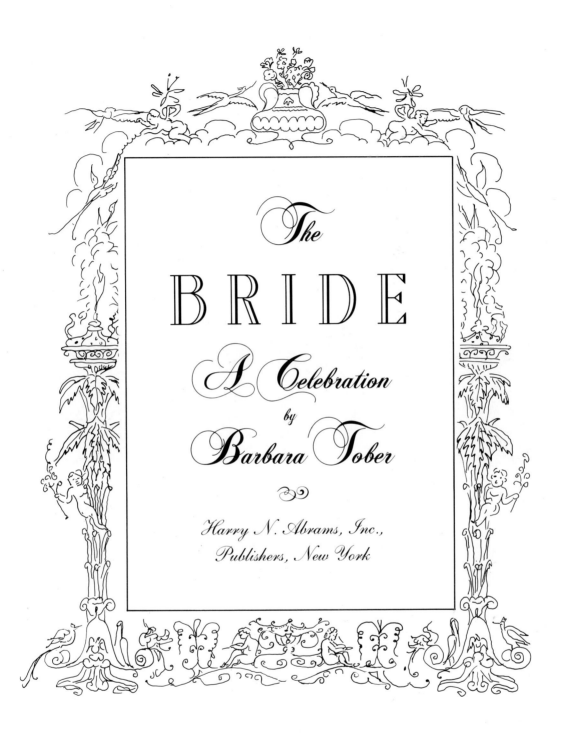

The

BRIDE

A Celebration

by

Barbara Tober

Harry N. Abrams, Inc.,
Publishers, New York

Project Manager: Darlene Geis
Editor: Kathie Ness
Designer: Judith Henry

Library of Congress Cataloging in Publication Data
Tober, Barbara. The bride.
1. Courtship. 2. Weddings. 3. Marriage customs
and rites. I. Title.
HQ801.T55 1984   392'.5   84-420
ISBN 0-8109-0737-2

Published in 1984 by Harry N. Abrams, Incorporated, New York

Printed and bound in Japan

To Donald,

whose love and support

have been my inspiration since

that very first day

Contents

Foreword

Throughout the lives of all women—in childhood dreams and adult fantasies—there floats the vision of a bride. This reverie, dramatized in song and history, myth and folklore, is rooted among the most primitive and ennobling aspirations of humanity: the need for romance, fidelity, eternal love, and immortality. The dream is universal, yet no two marriages are alike.

Today, as in no other time in history, husband and wife can create the kind of married lifestyle that suits *them,* individually as well as together. Those newly launched into the mysteries of wedded partnership quickly discover that only humor and tolerance can smooth the sometimes jagged edges of human imperfection. Others with a long and enviable history of happiness become a beacon to the uninitiated, though they themselves may be reflecting all the while on their own coming to terms with reality. No one outside their private world can measure what endless reserves of energy and nourishment each partner can draw from the other, what strength can be built on such an intimate bond, what resolve can come from such total commitment.

The bride celebrates her faith in the future with a joyous feast and joins her bridegroom on a journey of passion and dedication. Theirs is the story of the ages, yet each marriage is unique. This "rite of passage," unequaled by any other, is a moment to be celebrated by friends and relatives close to the couple, and even by those who are not privileged to know them well. Marriage is a reaffirmation of optimism and belief in the continuation of the family . . . so for the bride, the wedding is only the beginning.

Barbara Tober

1

The Bride: Her Special Mystique

Wedding bells peal. A radiant bride appears, on the arm of her exuberant groom. As they make their way to a waiting car, guests, flurrying behind them, snap pictures, throw rice, offer congratulations and good wishes, and shed tears of happiness. There's an excitement, an electricity, a magic in the air. Even strangers passing by smile and call out, "Good luck!" as the couple drives off.

The bride is fantasy made real, innocence made personal, promise made possible. She is the central figure in a universal ritual—the wedding—which is planned for, participated in, and celebrated all over the world. Family, friends, even casual observers who witness a marriage are deeply stirred by the occasion. They look at a couple, but they see a bride. She might be twenty, forty, or seventy; dressed in homespun cotton, French lace, or embroidered silk. She might be Japanese, Egyptian, or Mexican. She might be married in a cathedral, on a mountaintop, or in front of an exotic shrine. She is, was, always will be a symbol of hope, love, beauty, and a cultural ideal. She restores our faith in life.

Why? Because marriage is a coming together not only of two people but of two families, sometimes two communities or two countries, a bonding of the family of mankind. It is a symbol of continuity—a landmark that signifies the past as well as the future. Each person attending a wedding not only thinks of the couple's future, but is also poignantly reminded of the passage of time.

OPPOSITE *The rapturous ride from ceremony to reception becomes a royal spectacular with Princess Diana and Prince Charles.*

In *Fiddler on the Roof* the parents of the bride sing with the chorus:

> *Is this the little girl I carried?*
> *Is this the little boy at play?*
> *I don't remember growing older,*
> *When did they?*

Of course, the image of the bride evokes more than nostalgia—she represents the spark of a new beginning and the assurance that there is a plan and harmony in the world.

Marriage by Capture

In the earliest days, a man seeking a wife simply captured her and dragged her away. He selected her not for her beauty or tenderness, but for her potential as a good worker and breeder of additional workers. And although love may not have been the first incentive for the capture, perhaps some stirring of a feeling not unlike love may have developed with time.

"My husband was good, tender, generous . . . and strange as it may seem, I loved him," explained Mary Jemison, who was captured by the Shawnee Indians in 1755 and was married to a Delaware Indian at age seventeen.

Gradually marriage by capture became a courtship game. Even today, when a male Eskimo tries to "steal" a woman, a mock battle between them ensues in which the woman proves her worth by putting up a fight. Her mother keeps a close eye on the proceedings to be sure that her daughter shows enough self-esteem to resist fiercely.

An old Australian aborigine custom is similar. The intended groom runs away with his chosen

Marriage by capture, performed here by impassioned Tartar horsemen.

bride. Her father and brothers follow in close pursuit. If the couple can find a place to hide, and if the kidnapped bride is lucky enough to be pregnant by the time the family finally catches up with them, the game ends and the man and woman are considered married.

But if the bride is not yet pregnant, the script calls for her kinsmen to poke the poor girl in the legs and feet with a spear and take her home. Then the couple run off again, and again are pursued and captured. This continues until the bride's mother is convinced that her daughter's worth has been well established by the ritual. When mother decrees, "Better let him have her," the game ends.

Arranged Marriages

For the bride today, to say "I do" is to make a very personal statement. But marriage is not only a private declaration of love; it is also a public commitment, a social contract witnessed and endorsed by the community.

Until relatively recently, marriage was purely an economic transaction, a practical merger of labor and property between two families, rather than an expression of love and romance between two individuals. As an old German saying goes, "It is not man that marries maid, but field marries field, vineyard marries vineyard, cattle marry cattle." Often a man could increase his property through a marriage alliance. There were two ways to gain advantage in a world where land and wealth were synonymous. Either one fought to win the next acre . . . or one married it.

Arranged marriages were a traditional means of controlling who married whom, thereby ensuring that the union of bride and groom would enhance family wealth and status. Royal marriages were also arranged for political reasons, with the wedding a sort of flesh-and-blood treaty to unite or

*The ritual of marriage was not always tender or sweet. These women of Venice
found themselves unwilling brides to overpowering grooms.*

King Tutankhamen and Queen Ankhesenamon depicted in gold.

A twelfth-century priest marries this couple by joining their hands.

This finely crafted etching captures the moment of another royal wedding—the marriage of Henry VII.

expand empires. Princesses from one country were advised to marry royalty from another, in order to forge political alliances and strengthen their homelands. And in the nineteenth century, less momentous arranged marriages helped to ex-pand the American frontier when mail-order brides became available to hard-working bache-lors in the sparsely populated western states.

Parents still arrange marriages in many parts of China, India, Africa, Japan, and in some Moslem and Jewish communities. Indian and Japanese newspapers publish matrimonial want-ads—one respectable family looking for another so that their children can wed. One thriving mail-order service that specializes in Japanese brides claims it receives more than 5,000 letters from would-be husbands each year. Another report says that about 3,000 Philippine women recently emi-grated to Australia and West Germany, and an

Few introductions could cause more nervousness than the miai, *or arranged meeting. To an American or a European,
the sequence of the courtship of this Japanese couple seems reversed: having committed
themselves to the intimacy of marriage, they have now been brought together to become acquainted.*

She vows to love who vowed to rule—(the chosen at her side)
Let none say, God preserve the queen! but rather, Bless the bride!
None blow the trump, none bend the knee, none violate the dream
Wherein no monarch but a wife she to herself may seem.
Or if ye say, Preserve the queen! oh, breathe it inward low—
She is a woman, and beloved! and 't is enough but so.

      Elizabeth Barrett Browning, "Crowned and Wedded,"
      on the marriage of Queen Victoria

Prince Rahotep and his wife, Nofret, preserved in painted limestone. The statues come from Rahotep's tomb.

in the agrarian economy that prevailed before the Industrial Revolution (they could work and bear children), the groom or his father paid a bride-price, or bridewealth, to the bride's father to

A Seminole Indian bride and groom, c. 1895.

additional 4,000 traveled to Europe and the United States, after mail-order introductions.

How was a wife traditionally acquired in the old days? The fathers of the bride and groom, or a hired go-between, usually made the arrangements. Since young women were a financial asset

---

The More, The Better

In the old days, affluent men could afford to marry many wives. To prove his status, King Solomon had 700 wives and 300 concubines. Akbar the Great, sixteenth-century emperor of Hindustan, recommended that each man should have at least four wives: "a Hindu to bear children, a Persian for conversation, an Afghan to keep house, and a Turk to beat up as an example to the other three."

Polygamy was also a common practice in societies where women outnumbered men, who were often killed hunting or waging war; women were dependent upon men, and sharing a husband was considered better than having no husband at all. Besides, as a Chinese sage pointed out, one teapot could fill many cups, but who has ever seen many teapots for just one cup?

Nevertheless, polyandry—the custom of one woman marrying numerous men—was allowed in a few ancient societies where women were in short supply. Where polyandry existed, however, the woman did not have the right to select her husbands, but rather she was shared among men who agreed to treat her as their common wife.

This engraving of a wedding procession in Persia displays the pageantry of the event.

make up for the loss of his daughter and her services. Money or work was legal tender. Often the betrothal was confirmed while the girl was still young, so that the bride's family could reap the economic and social benefits during the years preceding the wedding.

This is exemplified in the Old Testament story of Jacob, who was required to work seven years for Laban in order to marry Laban's daughter Rachel. Love-struck Jacob toiled especially hard to earn his wife. But after the wedding ceremony, he discovered that he had actually married Leah, her elder sister. This, Laban explained, was necessary because elder daughters must marry first. Jacob dutifully celebrated the bridal week (an ancient wedding lasted for seven days of festivities), and then began another seven years of labor to win the girl he really wanted for his wife. This time, mercifully, he was able to marry Rachel first and work later.

Although females were regarded as possessions to be passed from father to husband, the aura

Marriage has more often symbolized the merging of political parties, properties, or wealth than it has symbolized a romantic commitment.

Adam and Eve found it easy to fall in love; they were made for each other.

Chagall's romantic painting, The Bride and Groom of the Eiffel Tower.

This bride was actually "worth her weight in gold."

tom of a dowry began in Europe sometime after 500 B.C. The husband benefited from the dowry as long as he and his wife were married. But if the husband died or the marriage was dissolved, the bride had her dowry to fall back on—unless it had been dissipated. The dowry was supposed to ensure that the bride could maintain herself without a husband if the need arose.

"Matchmaker, Matchmaker . . ." In any exchange of money and goods, the middleman flourishes. And throughout history, bride-price and dowry negotiations have proved no exception. In Brittany, until about 1850, two intermediaries called *bazvalans,* who represented the bridegroom, would visit the bride's family one night. Her mother would show approval of the match by lighting a welcoming fire. The bazvalans would extol the virtues of the bridegroom with such exaggeration and hyperbole that the mother, or

surrounding the bride was nevertheless romantic. For the bride was clearly valuable—whether for her ability to work, her beauty, or her capacity to produce children. The man who selected her for his wife followed the elaborate courtship behavior required by their culture. Perhaps he delivered cows, weapons, or crops, worked in the fields, or joined the bride's male relatives as an ally, even if only to socialize. By performing these rituals, he confirmed her worth.

The esteem in which the bride was held was heightened by her dowry—the land, money, or household goods she brought with her. The cus-

In the Orient, as in many parts of the world, matchmakers thrived. These Oriental marriage negotiators sometimes played a more active role in the destiny of the couple than the man or woman did.

When love became devotion instead of possession, marriage reached the climax of its slow ascent from brutality.

Will Durant

even the grandmother, would jokingly offer herself up to this paragon of manhood! Finally the bazvalans, dressed in red and purple stockings, would escort the eager bridegroom to visit his young lady. When the couple ate from the same plate, the negotiations were sealed.

In Turkey the initial go-between was the bridegroom's mother. She inspected prospective brides as they paraded nude in the public baths and gave detailed reports to her son.

Have these customs changed? Not really. For instance, even in the 1980s potential brides and grooms in Japan meet through the services of a go-between who arranges a "chance" meeting. If the couple's reactions are positive, the negotiations proceed. If not, they are dropped and neither person is placed in an embarrassing position. Today, in the United States and in Japan, computers have also taken on this matchmaking role. Individuals are paired according to a long list of data—and the chance meeting now often takes place via the video screen.

ABOVE The Wedding of Tsarevna Elena the Fair, *an enchanting version of the ceremony based on a Russian fairy tale.*
BELOW *The artless figures on this decorative plate reflect the joyful emotion of a Hawaiian wedding.*

Victorian postcards.

Fertility Rites and the Bride

"First comes love, then comes marriage, / then comes [Anna] with a baby carriage," goes the old jingle.

The bride traditionally symbolizes a hope for future generations, a continuation of the family name and lineage. For until recently, children followed marriage as night follows day.

It's not surprising, therefore, that weddings abound in fertility symbols, most of which relate to the bride. In early human history, men probably did not understand that they had anything to do with the mysterious changes that took place in their women, followed by the remarkable arrival of babies. As long as that naiveté persisted, women were treated like mysterious goddesses

The bride holds a bouquet, traditional symbol of fertility.

A future bride plays her make-believe role in borrowed finery.

who magically produced children if the procreative spirits were duly propitiated.

In ancient days, silver coins were placed in the bride's shoe to appease Diana, the goddess of chastity and unmarried maidens, so that the bride could lose her virginity and bear a child. Breaking an object during the wedding—such as a coconut in India or a piece of pottery in Russia—symbolized the breaking of the bride's hymen, which would lead to conception. In Persia, the bride

The couple leaving the church pass through a shower of rice, an age-old symbol of fruitfulness.

herself broke a hen's egg against a wall, while keeping her face turned toward Mecca. (The Jewish glass-breaking tradition, however, is a symbol of the destruction of the temple of Jerusalem.) The noise of all this breakage not only heightened the spirit of revelry at the wedding but was also meant to confuse any evil spirits lurking about. It was intended that nothing should harm the bride or impede the main purpose of the union.

The bride understood the meaning of these rituals. She knew there were great expectations for her marriage. The gathered assemblage needed her to accept her sexuality and childbearing responsibilities for the continuance of the race. And, recognizing the inherent dangers, they wished her Godspeed.

Today brides still carry a bouquet of flowers, signifying life, growth, fertility. And throughout the world the new bride and groom are showered with whatever foodstuff is plentiful: in India and America with rice, in France with wheat, in Morocco with raisins, figs, and dates. The hope is that the couple will be as fruitful as the earth that bore this provender.

This early twentieth-century bridegroom gazes down at his new bride with hopeful
visions of children and family. Pioneering Harlem photographer James van der Zee's double exposure
tenderly pictures this couple's dream.

When Daisy Mae finally got her man, it was
stunning news—another version of marriage by capture.

What greater thing is there for two human souls
than to feel that they are joined for life—to
strengthen each other in all labor, to rest on
each other in all sorrow, to minister to each
other in all pain, to be one with each other in
silent, unspeakable memories at the moment of
the last parting.

George Eliot

The Fascination of the Bride

Just as in medieval villages, where the bride's al-
lure drew the interest, attention, and admiration
of the townsfolk, so in today's society—despite
modern cynicism—the bride evokes a special excitement.

The adulation of the bride today extends not
only to celebrities who march down the aisle—

although almost nothing sells newspapers like a
front-page story about Elizabeth Taylor's plans
to wed yet again—but even to fictional characters
who marry. In 1974, 40 million television view-
ers watched the *Rhoda* segment in which Rhoda
Morgenstern, Mary's longtime friend on the
Mary Tyler Moore Show, finally became a bride.
And in 1952, when, after years of trying, Al
Capp's cartoon character Daisy Mae Scragg actually got L'il Abner to Marryin' Sam, it made
the cover of *Life* magazine.

The marriage of Prince Charles and Princess
Diana in 1980 was the international media event
of the decade, summoning up for most of the
world all the feelings of awe, delight, romance,
and expectation that are inspired by every bride
on her wedding day. The Most Rev. Robert Run-

OPPOSITE *The fantasy bride, this one in cloth of gold
with a nimbus of tulle, is the traditional grand finale
of every fashion show.*

Senator and Mrs. John F. Kennedy: a famous marriage that was celebrated across the United States.

> When the wedding march sounds its resolute approach, the clock no longer ticks; it tolls the hour.... The figures in the aisle are no longer individuals; they symbolize the human race.
>
> Anne Morrow Lindbergh, *Dearly Beloved*

cie, the Archbishop of Canterbury, who married the royal pair, spoke of the public aspect of marriage.

Any marriage which is turned in upon itself, in which the bride and groom simply gaze obsessively at one another, goes sour after a time.

A marriage which really works is one which works for others. Marriage has both a private face and a public importance. If we solved all our economic problems and failed to build loving families, it would profit us nothing, because the family is the place where the future is created good and full of love—or deformed.

Those who are married live happily ever after the wedding day if they persevere in the real adventure, which is the royal task of creating each other and creating a more loving world.

Queen Elizabeth, a few years earlier, spoke of the way communal ties nurture a marriage.

A marriage begins by joining man and wife together, but this relationship between two people, however deep at the time, needs to develop and mature with the passing years. For

The Wedding *1962–63. A striking bride and groom by Pop artist Marisol.*

that it must be held firm in the web of family relationships between parents and children, between grandparents and grandchildren, between cousins, aunts and uncles.

2
Romance and Betrothal

Love (Middle English, from the Old English *lufu* . . . Latin *lubere, libere* to please) . . . (1): strong affection for another arising out of kinship or personal ties . . . (2): attraction based on sexual desire : affection and tenderness felt by lovers.

(Webster's New Collegiate Dictionary)

Somehow the dictionary definition just doesn't capture the true essence of the word "love." Yet few people are able to describe it any better. They can recognize the delicious symptoms: an inability to eat or sleep, a lightheaded feeling, contentedness with the world at large, a tingling all over . . . but when it comes to explaining the divine affliction, they're at a loss.

Love is consuming, deceptive, exciting, wonderful. Everyone knows it when they see it (or so they hope); yet even in the grip of the emotion, they ask themselves the popular songwriter's question, "What Is This Thing Called Love?"

Philosophers, poets, artists, and musicians have tried to answer the same question:

José Ortega y Gasset, the Spanish philosopher, put it this way: "Love is that splendid triggering of human vitality . . . the supreme activity which nature affords anyone for going out of himself toward something else . . . the march of our inner being toward another . . . as if we were torn from our own vital depths and lived transplanted."

German philosopher Friedrich Wilhelm Nietzsche came up with: "Love is the state in which man sees things most widely different from what they are. The force of illusion reaches its zenith here."

Geoffrey Chaucer gave this illusion another name. "Love is blynd," he stated simply.

What picture does love bring to mind? A couple, of course. "Love consists in this, that two solitudes protect and touch and greet each other," wrote Rainer Maria Rilke in *Letters to a Young Poet.*

Somewhat less poetically, humorist Franklin Jones said: "Love doesn't make the world go 'round. Love is what makes the ride worthwhile."

And when two lovers meet, how do they feel? Humorist Henry Wheeler Shaw's Josh Billings, perhaps suffering from an affair of the heart, put it this way: "Love iz like the meazles; we kant have it bad but onst, and the later in life we have it the tuffer it goes with us."

Happy as everyone would be to come down with it, the fact remains that true love is a lot harder to catch than the common cold. François, duc de la Rochefoucauld, put his finger on it when he said, "True love is like ghosts, which everybody talks about and few have seen."

But with all this confusion over the meaning of love, Emily Dickinson's lines stand clear:

> That love is all there is
> Is all we know of love.

Falling in Love

Falling in love is the most exciting part of any relationship. It may take a while—a 1970 study shows that love at first sight is pretty rare—but the fun's in the falling. According to the study, thirty percent of men couldn't say for sure whether or not they were in love until after the twentieth date, while forty-three percent of

OPPOSITE *Two lovers from another age stare into each other's eyes and for a moment, or an hour, or a lifetime, nothing else in the world matters.*

36

There is only one situation I can think of in which men and women make an effort to read better than they usually do. When they are in love and reading a love letter, they read for all they are worth. They read every word three ways; they read between the lines and in the margins. . . . They may even take the punctuation into account. Then, if never before or after, they read.

Mortimer Adler

NATHANIEL HAWTHORNE TO SOPHIA PEABODY

Dearest,—I wish I had the gift of making rhymes, for methinks there is poetry in my head and heart since I have been in love with you. You are a Poem. Of what sort, then? Epic? Mercy on me, no! A sonnet? No; for that is too labored and artificial. You are a sort of sweet, simple, gay, pathetic ballad, which Nature is singing, sometimes with tears, sometimes with smiles, and sometimes with intermingled smiles and tears.

ZELDA SAYRE TO F. SCOTT FITZGERALD

Scott—there's nothing in all the world I want but you—and your precious love—All material things are nothing. . . . and I'd do anything— anything—to keep your heart for my own—I don't want to live—I want to love first and live incidentally. . . . Don't you think I was made for you? I feel like you had me ordered—and I was delivered to you.

JOHN ADAMS TO ABIGAIL SMITH

Miss Adorable
By the same Token that the Bearer hereof satt up with you last night I hereby order you to give him, as many Kisses, and as many Hours of your Company after 9 O'clock as he shall please to Demand and charge them to my Account: This Order, or Requisition call it which you will is in Consideration of a similar order Upon Aurelia for the like favour, and I presume I have good Right to draw upon you for the Kisses as I have given two or three Millions at least, when one has been received, and of Consequence the Account between us is immensely in favour of

yours,
John Adams

NAPOLEON TO JOSEPHINE

I have not spent a day without loving you; I have not spent a night without embracing you. . . . In the midst of my duties, whether I am at the head of my army or inspecting the camps, my beloved Josephine stands alone in my heart, occupies my mind, fills my thoughts.

and previous marriages did not figure as important considerations.

And what does the bride-to-be look for in her choice of a man? In a *Psychology Today* survey, women overwhelmingly voted for a man with the ability to love (ninety-six percent mentioned this). A close second was a man with a willingness to stand up for his own beliefs. Eighty-nine percent of women opted for a man with warmth and eighty-six percent called for self-confidence in their men. Gentleness was a highly ranked trait also: eighty-six percent of the women surveyed were looking for this quality, so devastatingly attractive when combined with masculine strength.

With 4,677,000,000 people in the world today (232,600,000 in the United States alone), the prospect of finding the needle of true love in the haystack of overpopulation seems a bit overwhelming. Books like *Playgirl's Little Black Book*, *The American Bachelor Registry*, and *America's Richest Bachelors* are aimed at helping would-be brides find a life-mate.

For those who prefer to choose their love object in person, there are singles groups, computer dating companies, video dating services, vacation get-togethers for bachelors and bachelorettes. For every age, occupation, and interest, there's a matchmaking group. It is also possible to advertise for mates in magazines and newspapers. The ads are usually brief and to the point: "Comely Petite—very well read, financially secure, seeks Jewish gent, 55–60, well-spoken, caring." Those who fit the description are encouraged to write to a box number. Advertisers are not so different from the clients of matchmakers who arranged marriages—they are still looking for wealth, health, intelligence, common interests and backgrounds.

women, evidently the more cautious sex, felt the same way. Over the course of a lifetime, men claim to experience "true love" an average of 1.2 times, women 1.3 times.

What is it men look for in a potential mate? A *Redbook* magazine survey reports that eighty-five percent of the men questioned were searching for a woman who would love them. Eighty percent considered intelligence the most important trait in the woman of their dreams. Seventy percent were *still* on the lookout for a woman with good legs, and sixty-five percent demanded a sense of humor. Self-confidence in a woman was important to forty-seven percent of the men questioned. Thirty-eight percent were only willing to consider a woman with slim hips and a shapely rear. Some things never change! Interestingly, age

La Gamme d'Amour (The Gamut of Love). *Music weaves its magic in this seventeenth-century painting by Antoine Watteau.*

The office also is an increasingly popular spot for romance. As women enter the labor force in larger numbers than ever, the workplace has more and more become a meeting place, a first stop on the road to the altar.

"If Music Be the Food of Love . . ."

Serenading has always been an ornament of courtship. Indian braves from the upper Mississippi played a flutelike instrument outside the wigwam of a beloved squaw, hoping for her favorable attentions. In modern days, it is more likely that a suitor will sing to his sweetheart under her college dorm window. Everything from mariachi music and guitar solos to recorders and kazoos have been called into service. Music offers a romantic backdrop to courtship; the record player and tape deck have soothed the ears and sensibilities of many a modern inamorata.

In the 1940s, big band music, touch dancing, and romantic movies featuring Fred Astaire and Ginger Rogers put couples in the mood for love. In the 1950s, rock 'n roll enthusiasts were "sent" by Elvis Presley's "Love Me Tender" and

Mr. Darcy (Laurence Olivier) bestows an elegant kiss on the hand of a cool Elizabeth Bennett (Greer Garson) in the movie Pride and Prejudice.

"Hound Dog." Then came the Beatles with "I Wanna Hold Your Hand" and "Love Me Do." The 1970s and '80s brought new waves of sound for lovers—in rock, disco, country, and punk. However frenetic the style, the love songs of the time have always managed to make young people's hearts beat faster.

"A Kiss Is But a Kiss"

Ah, the kiss! Anthropologists speculate that the kiss developed by accident—a couple affectionately rubbing noses probably slipped and discovered the thrill of lips touching lips! Then again, it may have originated from the furry ancestors of humans—monkeys—who smack their lips during foreplay and occasionally brush mouths during copulation. As they evolved, so did the kiss.

The kiss also figures prominently in the Bible, particularly in the Old Testament's "Song of Songs." This voluptuous celebration of the union of a bride and her groom begins, "Let him kiss me with the kisses of his mouth."

No one may know when the custom started—but the kiss has blazed an incendiary trail through the pages of history. Paris, prince of Troy, precipitated the ten-year Trojan War when he dared to kiss Menelaus's wife and became so enthralled by Helen that he had to have her for his own. Cleopatra's kisses have been famous for centuries—historians say they destroyed Mark Antony and probably sealed the sorry fate of Rome.

The kiss has been a solemn part of the wedding ceremony since the days of the Roman Empire. It was the custom then to hold a betrothal ceremony in which the bride and groom kissed and joined right hands, after which the woman received a ring. The kiss was a legal bond. In fact, the kiss was the *only* legal bond—and if one of the engaged pair died before the wedding, the other could keep the presents only if the two had already kissed! Although a kiss is no longer a required part of the marriage ceremony, and some denominations don't even approve of the nuptial embrace, it is still a radiant moment when the bride's lips meet the groom's for the first time after they have been pronounced "man and wife."

Valentine from Milan, c. 1500

The Proposal

In the days of marriage by capture, there was no need to propose to the bride. A man simply dragged off the woman of his choice without a by-your-leave. Then came the era of arranged marriages and women still had little to say. The agreement was made between the families. Vestiges of this custom remained, and for years it was considered appropriate for the suitor to ask the bride's father for her hand. With today's less stringent social rules, however, a suitor not only doesn't have to seek permission to marry from his loved one's father, but the man may not even be the one who pops the question.

Another difference is that years ago, proposals were made more formally than they are today. In

"I'm not going to marry anyone who says, 'You gotta marry me, Howard.' I mean, the thing is if a woman wants me to marry her, she can at least say please.'"

"Please marry me, Howard. Please. Please."

William Inge, *Picnic*

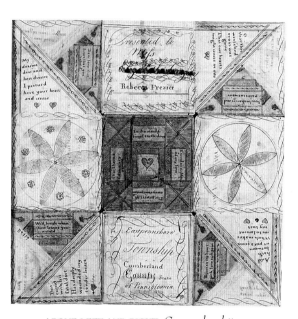

ABOVE LEFT AND RIGHT *German love letters,*
c. 1800–40, from Pennsylvania
BELOW *Cutwork love letter, c. 1779, from Pennsylvania*

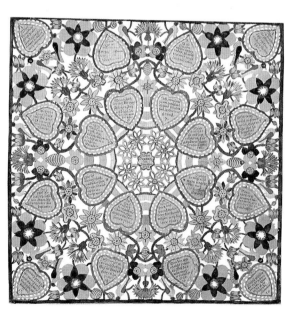

the nineteenth century, instead of the traditional "Will you marry me?" proposals were more likely to be statements that announced the suitor's feelings without any request for betrothal. Once the declaration of love was made, it was tantamount to asking for the girl's hand.

Proposals have changed with the times, as the following example from Jane Austen's *Pride and Prejudice* illustrates. The proud Darcy admits to Elizabeth Bennett:

> "In vain have I struggled. It will not do. My feelings will not be repressed. You must allow me to tell you how ardently I admire and love you. . . ."

He concluded with representing to her the strength of that attachment which, in spite of

Der Küss (The Kiss), *Gustave Klimt, 1907–8*

Marriage...hath in it less of beauty but more of safety than the single life; it hath more care, but less danger; it is more merry and more sad, is fuller of sorrows and fuller of joys; it lies under more burdens, but is supported by all the strengths of love and charity, and those burdens are delightful.

Jeremy Taylor

all his endeavors, he had found impossible to conquer; and with expressing his hope that it would now be rewarded by her acceptance of his hand. As he said this she could easily see that he had no doubt of a favorable answer.

Proposals have been emblazoned across cakes, tucked inside fortune cookies, etched in the sand, written in the sky, placed in newspaper ads, sent via Western Union and carrier pigeon, broadcast in letters five feet high on a rented billboard. Like the answer to the magic question in a fairy tale, the right answer to a proposal has the power of transformation. It can turn an everyday woman into a bride.

Spreading the News

Naturally, when two people become engaged they want everyone to share their joy. And so they announce their intentions to friends and relatives. There may also be a requirement that the banns be published, to make sure that there are no legal objections to the impending marriage.

The act of engagement may be symbolized by a ring, a kiss, or even the sharing of food or drink. In the Middle Ages, drinking a glass of wine or other alcoholic beverage with a member of the opposite sex signaled an engagement. In colonial America, two people who shared food in the kitchen were thought to be engaged. Today we still celebrate an engagement with a toast to the happy couple's healthy and prosperous future.

Parental consent or approval has been of varied importance over the years. In colonial America, a girl was allowed to marry at the age of twelve without parental permission. Life spans were

An old-fashioned Flemish couple modestly clasp hands to indicate their betrothal.

Clandestine romance is hauntingly portrayed in Henri Rousseau's Rendezvous in the Forest.

much shorter then and early marriages were necessary. In every state in America now the legal marriage age is considerably higher than twelve—a reflection of the longer future which awaits the married couple.

Today an announcement is often published in the town hall, local newspapers, or church bulletin. Couples sometimes have their own unique ways of breaking the news to friends and relatives.

One couple sent a cake to their parents with "We're Engaged!" written on it. Another couple sent postcards with their photo to all their friends with the news of the engagement on the back.

One way to announce the engagement is at an engagement party. Betrothals were once marked by a party called a "flouncing," where the starry-eyed couple met with their future in-laws. From this moment on, the engagement was official.

The Wisdom of Gems

EMERALD   Contains the key to domestic bliss and success in love. Cleopatra wore emeralds from her own mine.

RUBY   "The sun's own gem" is said to house a warm flame. Considered a sign of love, it is a favorite for engagements. According to legend, the ruby in an engagement ring will change color and darken if the course of true love is not running smoothly. If all is going well, it will be a lighter shade of red. The ruby is also said to ward off evil spirits and bad dreams.

AMETHYST   Means perfection according to biblical lore. The Greeks believed that amethysts had a sobering effect: the word is a combination of the Greek words for "not" and "to intoxicate." Believed to ensure a husband's love, it became a favorite gem among Roman women as a symbol of faithfulness and sincerity.

SAPPHIRE   The Persians believed that the earth was balanced on a sapphire, its reflection lending color to the sky. As a birthstone it stands for truth and faithfulness. Accord-ing to legend, it also brings good health and good fortune. Helen of Troy wore a sapphire, as does Princess Diana.

GARNET   Stands for constancy and true friendship. Accord-ing to Talmudic legend, Noah's Ark was lit by a large garnet. Folklore suggests that if you want someone to love you, you should give them a garnet.

DIAMOND   Considered a symbol of matrimonial happiness. It is said to endow the wearer with courage and to protect him or her from evil spirits. The diamond is also an emblem of innocence. Folklore has it that if a man wants to know whether his bride has been faithful, he need only hold a diamond over her head while she sleeps. Should she turn toward him, she is true, but if she turns away, she has been cheating. Folklore does not tell if the bride gets the diamond after passing the test.

AQUAMARINE   The person who wears this stone is said to be able to read another's thoughts. It is also believed to make the wearer more courageous and intelligent.

The bride-to-be could not be seen talking with another man, nor could the groom-to-be talk with another woman. There was no turning back after this social event. If a woman were to call off the engagement at this point, her fiancé would have the right to claim half of her worldly goods as his own. Similarly, if he were to renege, she would have the same rights to his property.

Today engagement parties are festive get-togethers, not irrevocable public and legal commitments. They may be formal or informal—a lavish cocktail party at a country club, a summer barbecue, or a small family dinner.

The Pledge of the Ring

Diamonds are forever . . . and so, one hopes, is the commitment of love which is symbolized by a

Our attachment to hands started in 1940, when Richard gave me a ring he had ordered especially made. It was a man's hand clasping a woman's hand, in two tones of gold. The hands could be unclasped, to show a ruby heart in the palm of the man. Over the years people have said, "But you can't see the heart, you wouldn't know it was there." We knew.

When he gave it to me, Richard described it as a "friendship ring." When we decided to get married and use it as a wedding ring, I remember telling him, "I think this is carrying friendship too far."

Mary Martin, *My Heart Belongs*

diamond ring. Though not every bride-to-be follows the custom of wearing an engagement ring today, it nevertheless remains a sign and symbol of betrothal, a formal covenant between two lovers, whether it is a diamond or another choice.

Rings have been with us since the beginning of time. The ancient Egyptians had them. The Romans used them. But how did they come to have more than just a decorative purpose? Why are they linked to the idea of engagement and marriage? Before the introduction of coinage, gold rings were circulated as currency. A man would give his bride a gold ring as a sign that he trusted

ABOVE *Lady Diana and Prince Charles:*
the engagement sapphire meets the royal signet.
BELOW *The classic American engagement ring,*
a diamond solitaire, lights up the prenuptial
interlude for a bride-to-be.

her with his property. Under Roman law, a bridegroom would furnish a ring as a sign of security, putting up collateral to protect the interests of the bride-to-be. Some believe that the idea of using a ring to seal the pact dates back to the time in Iceland when a marriage pledge was made by a man passing his hand through a large iron ring to clasp the hand of his beloved.

During the Elizabethan period and earlier, the *gimmal,* or interlocking set of rings, was extremely popular. During the engagement period one ring was worn by the groom, one by the bride, and one by a witness. At the time of the wedding, all three would be united on the bride's finger.

It was not until the nineteenth century that the diamond ring became popular for engagements. Sometimes jewels were used to spell "love," both figuratively and literally. A Victorian suitor might have a ring made up to spell "dearest" (diamond, emerald, amethyst, ruby, epidote, sapphire, and turquoise). Another popular combination was lapis lazuli, opal, verde antique, emerald, moonstone, and epidote, to spell "Love me." Today the diamond solitaire—a sign of wealth as well as imperishable devotion—is the most popular choice among American couples for an engagement ring.

In this age of sexual equality, engagement rings for men are gaining popularity. Perhaps there will soon be a return to the gimmal.

The symbolic ring, cartoon-style: The Ring, *1962, Roy Lichtenstein*

5

Engagement

An engaged couple not only feel different from the rest of us—as though set apart by their golden glow that is visible to all—they are also required to act differently, with a whole new set of rules to follow. Engagement behavior has always been strictly regulated, although it changes with the times, as illustrated by the etiquette experts of the day:

In the course of the next day the first of the usual betrothal visits were exchanged. The New York ritual was precise and inflexible in such matters; and in conformity with it Newland Archer first went with his mother and sister to call on Mrs. Welland, after which he and Mrs. Welland and May drove out to old Mrs. Manson Mingott's to receive the venerable ancestress' blessing.

(Edith Wharton,
The Age of Innocence, 1920)

As soon as they receive the news, all the relatives of the groom-elect must call on the bride. She is not "welcomed by the family" until their cards, left upon her in person, assure her so. She must, of course, return all of these visits, and as soon as possible.

(Emily Post,
The Blue Book of Social Usage, 1928)

Chaperonage is not a girl's lot today, but there are still a few wise rules best to observe. Even an engaged couple may not spend the night under the same roof without the presence of someone to chaperone them . . . must never do anything to cause talk or lower his or her esteem in the public mind. Hackneyed but true,

"Discretion is the better part of valor." Just being engaged doubles your visibility in the public eye.

(Bride's Magazine,
The Bride's Book of Etiquette, 1948)

When an engaged couple must travel unaccompanied overnight on a public conveyance, their accommodations should not be adjoining, and the presence of a chaperon would be in order at the destination. . . . Unmarried contemporaries are not considered suitable as chaperons, and an engaged pair traveling by automobile may not, with propriety, make overnight stops at hotels or motor inns, either by themselves or accompanied only by unmarried friends of the same age.

(Emily Post, *Etiquette*, 1969)

It is far better to think how much they [the engaged couple] may be bursting with physical desire for each other than to see them actually demonstrating it.

(Amy Vanderbilt,
Complete Book of Etiquette, 1978)

If your parents aren't acquainted with your fiancé yet, a letter or note asking them to please "invite someone very special" for a weekend or holiday works nicely. You needn't say anything until your fiancé feels comfortable and at home —rest assured, your parents will have a hint of your plans. (Incidentally, even if you are already sharing an apartment or house, you shouldn't expect to share a room in your parents' home if this makes them uneasy.)

(Bride's Magazine,
The New Bride's Book of Etiquette, 1981)

An outdoor wedding against a mountain background—the setting of the ceremony is one of the important choices engaged couples have to make.

The Best Time to Marry

A couple's engagement not only sets in motion a new code of courtship behavior, it also triggers what may seem like endless planning: choices and decisions to be made about every detail. Gone are the days when the groom's only job was to show up at the ceremony. Now both the bride and the groom think of the wedding day as a shared event.

Determining when to marry is usually the first major decision a couple must make—a choice that is fraught with mystical significance, superstitious peril, and religious tradition.

Since matrimony in its mystical origins was the work of the gods, the firmament—and the seasons that follow the stars—has always been a strong determining factor in decisions regarding the wedding date. June, the month claimed by Juno, Roman queen of heaven and goddess of femininity and marriage, has been the most popular. Although only by a small margin, it is still the month chosen most often by brides today.

But this was not always so. The calendar below gives the pros and cons for each month:

JANUARY   Ancient Greeks dedicated this month (named Gamelion for *gamos,* or consummation) to Hera, protectress of wives and fertility. Most Greek marriages took place in this "marriage month."

FEBRUARY   Anybody can fall in love in February, but a Catholic mustn't marry until after Lent, nor a Jew between the holidays of Passover and Shabuoth.

MARCH   "Marry in Lent, live to repent" still echoes in folklore, although the Eastern Orthodox Church, which forbids Lenten weddings, will perform simple ceremonies in wartime or in a case of dire emergency. March, named for the Roman god of war, might not augur well for a peaceful and affectionate marital career.

APRIL   Primitive peoples venerated the natural cycles of the earth, believing that the rebirth of spring aided human reproduction. As greenery and blossoms burst upon the land, so did weddings, which, it was hoped, would generate a rich harvest of offspring. The ancient Chinese gauged the best time for spring weddings by the first flowering of the peach blossoms.

MAY   "Marry in May, rue for aye" went a popular saying in Olde England. This tradition may hark back to the Lemuralia, Roman feasts of the dead, which took place in May. The Catholic Church dedicates the month of May to the Virgin Mary, patron saint of chastity. But many pagan Celts spent May in erotic revelry, making mockery of husbands and marital fidelity.

JUNE   Although the June bride made her debut in ancient Rome, the current preference for this month of the summer solstice has more pragmatic origins. June is the month of graduations, and before living together became commonplace, it was the natural choice of young couples starting out in the world and eager to face life together.

JULY AND AUGUST   Farm communities in the Middle Ages avoided the distraction of weddings before the crops were in. Practical husbandmen warned, "Never marry during harvest or you'll have no rest from worries and work." And, "They that wive between sickle and scythe shall never thrive," believed the Irish. Now that agriculture has become industrialized, such con-

When to Marry

Marry when the year is new,
Always loving, kind and true.
When February birds do mate,
You may wed, nor dread your fate.
If you wed when March winds blow,
Joy and sorrow both you'll know.
Marry in April when you can,
Joy for maiden and for man.
Marry in the month of May,
You will surely rue the day.
Marry when June roses blow,
Over land and sea you'll go.
They who in July do wed,
Must labour always for their bread.
Whoever wed in August be,
Many a change are sure to see.
Marry in September's shine,
Your living will be rich and fine.
If in October you do marry,
Love will come, but riches tarry.
If you wed in bleak November,
Only joy will come, remember.
When December's snows fall fast,
Marry and true love will last.

Traditional lines

straints are unnecessary, and July and August are among the most popular matrimonial months.

SEPTEMBER   The fall harvest moon was thought by peoples around the world to be a fertilizing influence, and farmers in Cambridgeshire, England, in the Ozark Mountains, and in certain areas of Germany still believe that a September moon shines luck—and good health—on a wedding celebration.

OCTOBER   Late October is ruled by Scorpio, astrological sign of the genitals, making it a propitious time to marry according to tradition in some rural areas of the United States.

A bride may wish for a sunny wedding day, but tradition has it that rain brings good luck.

NOVEMBER   With larders full and a cold winter coming, thoughts turn to home and hearth. Shetland Islanders consulted the omens on Halloween and celebrated the marriage shortly thereafter. Many Japanese marry in November because of the number of auspicious days on their astrological calendar.

DECEMBER   British brides were exhorted to avoid December, for "you always repent of marriage before the year is out." But many couples married on December 31 anyway, giving themselves the least possible amount of time to repent. Scottish lassies often chose December 31 so they could "ring out the old, ring in the new" with their husbands. And still others started the cycle all over again by marrying on New Year's Day.

People have also been at odds over what days of the week would prove auspicious. This popular rhyme was just one of many bits of advice for the bride-to-be to consider:

> *Monday for wealth,*
> *Tuesday for health,*
> *Wednesday best day of all,*
> *Thursday for losses,*
> *Friday for crosses,*
> *And Saturday, no luck at all.*

Friday was shadowed by being "hangman's day" in New England. Christians were averse to Sabbath revelry, fearing it would conflict with regular church services, so today most brides choose Saturday (also because it is the easiest day for most people to attend). Since Saturday is the Jewish Sabbath, Jews may not marry until after sundown or on Sunday.

And as for the time of day, in some lands, such

as Holland and Scotland, couples married as the tide—symbolizing the flow of riches and children —was rising. American brides often chose the cool of the evening or the hours before sunset for their ceremonies, especially in warm weather. But now, in this age of air conditioning and central heating, the time of the ceremony is usually determined by the type of ceremony and reception the couple chooses to have—early enough for a honeymoon getaway, late enough for candlelight, midafternoon for guests arriving from a distance.

Where and How

Ask any young woman and she can probably close her eyes and describe in vivid detail her ideal wedding scene: whitewashed walls and stained-glass windows . . . lush garden foliage ruffled by a gentle breeze . . . a city restaurant in the sky . . . a stately nineteenth-century church. For every bride, a good part of the pleasure of planning a wedding is choosing, or even creating, a setting that has seemed magical to her since childhood, or perhaps deciding on one that has romantic associations for the couple. There are picturesque spots throughout the United States, varied enough to make every wedding wish come true.

- The verdant rolling hills of Westbury Gardens on Long Island.
- Mission San José in San Antonio, where the wedding music might be a mariachi band.
- My Old Kentucky Home State Park in Bardstown, Kentucky, with its massive pillars and hanging ferns.
- Six thousand feet up at Timberline Lodge on Mount Hood in Oregon.

Simplicity is a most endearing quality, perhaps best conveyed by the serenity of this Quaker wedding.

No matter where the wedding ceremony is held, a bride will usually choose one of these ways to marry:

A religious service Each of the major religions celebrates the wedding with its own blend of tradition and doctrine. Most Protestant sects follow the familiar service from the Book of Common Prayer ("Dearly Beloved, we are gathered here in the sight of God . . ."). Quaker

Two ceremonies on a grand scale: (above) a Rothschild wedding, (right) a wedding in a cathedral.

brides and grooms may marry at home or in the local meetinghouse; they observe the traditional Quaker silence before reciting their vows, and all guests sign the marriage certificate. Mormons are wed "for time and eternity," rather than "until death do us part." For Catholics, several conferences with a priest precede the wedding; the bride is escorted down the aisle by her father, and the service stresses the permanence of the marriage bond. After the parents of a Jewish bride and groom take part in the processional, the couple is wed under a *huppah,* an ornamented canopy symbolizing shelter.

At home or outdoors Marrying at home affords the bride a setting that is truly personal, as she and her groom recite their vows in front of a stately fireplace or plant-filled bay window. Or the ceremony can be outdoors, amid blossoms and trees, perhaps with a bubbling brook nearby. Everything from an altar to a hundred chairs can be transported to the outdoor wedding site, while the bride and groom keep their fingers crossed for sunshine—and hire a tent in case of rain!

The home wedding might be a traditional religious service, or the couple might write portions of their own religious or civil ceremony.

A civil ceremony   Brief and to the point, this satisfies all the legal requirements without the frills. Each state decides who may perform a civil ceremony. Usually a justice of the peace, judge, or magistrate is authorized to say, "By virtue of the power invested in me, I now pronounce you man and wife."

A double wedding   This classic variation offers twice the splendor at half the expense. Most brides who double up are sisters—sharing a wedding can be an expression of fondness as well as an economical option for the parents. Double weddings are usually quite formal, with many attendants and many guests.

Sabres are raised in salute to this couple married
at the Cadet Chapel, West Point.

"WHEN YOU SAID YOU WANTED A DOUBLE WEDDING, I JUST
ASSUMED THERE'D BE ANOTHER COUPLE INVOLVED."

A military wedding   The bride who marries a commissioned officer on active duty may enjoy the pomp of a military service. Her bridegroom and his fellow officers/ushers appear in full dress uniform, and the recessional is climaxed by the couple walking under the famous arch of sabers (or swords in the case of the Navy). Military chapels at West Point, Annapolis, and the Air Force Academy can provide a handsome backdrop for this type of wedding.

Elopement   With or without the fabled ladder at the window, the young woman who dreams of eloping fantasizes about a figure of romance and daring who will carry her off to the nuptial bed. Real-life elopement is usually far less dramatic. Most couples who go this route wish either to marry quickly or to avoid all the commotion of a big wedding.

*For an older couple, well established, a marriage ceremony in the mayor's private office at City Hall,
as in this 1876 engraving, is a dignified and prestigious beginning of a new life.*

Wedding Money

Three hundred people drinking his champagne.
Three hundred people eating his food. Three
hundred. . . . He was ruined. Clearly and ut-
terly ruined.

(Edward Streeter, *Father of the Bride*)

In 1983 an article in the *Wall Street Journal*
announced that "wedding parties get bigger and
fancier as spending loosens up," and went on to
support the facts with examples from across the
country. Yet deciding how to allocate funds for
the various aspects of this pageant takes the skills
of a seasoned diplomat, a strong stomach, and a
steady hand (for writing checks). The result, how-

ever, is considered well worth the effort, especially
when judicious compromises linking fantasy and
reality eventually benefit everyone involved.

Average wedding costs today hover just around
the $6,000 mark. But the word "average" some-
how does not recognize the prime determining
factor for these emotionally charged financial decisions: passion!

Passion chooses antique lace, anemones and
wild mushrooms out of season, imported champagne, and a honeymoon on a yacht. Of course,
there have been a few frugal souls who have kept
strict tabs on the bottom line from beginning to
end. But it's a rare wedding that doesn't succumb
to an extravagance or two—even under the most
watchful and parsimonious eye.

Of course, the father of the bride may have

Another of the unlimited possibilities for ceremony settings: exchanging vows on the deck of a ship overlooking a tropical port.

waited his entire life to make a grand impression on his friends and family. This day is his opportunity, and whether he must withdraw substantial savings or simply deplete his checking account, he is proud of his single, undiluted, and unilateral ability to throw the party of a lifetime.

• One tobacco mogul turned his Beverly Hills home into a southern plantation for his daughter's wedding by having millions of magnolia blossoms glued to the trees, then banking the ceremony site—the library—with thousands of orchids and roses.

• Another proud father, who already *had* a southern plantation, floated a thousand gardenias in the swimming pool and commissioned gardens of assorted spring flowers to be planted around the outdoor wedding site.

• Middle-class Japanese families spend an average of $26,000 for a wedding (which means that some people—and not only heads of state or tycoons—spend much more). The bride and groom might descend from the ceiling amid dry-ice clouds, the bride changes costume as many as four times (twice in traditional wedding kimono and twice in Western dress), and hundreds of guests feast on lobster and ice cream. Money is the most popular wedding gift and much of it goes to the parents of both couples to help defray the costs.

• $1.5 million for a wedding? That's what was spent in 1950 when Princess Rajendar Kunwar married Prince Fatehsinha Gaekwar in Jodphur, India. One of the last displays of Indian royal pageantry, the guest list included some 54 maharajas, 55 lesser princes, 306 nobles, and 4,500 lower-ranking guests and servants.

These are the ultra-extravagant weddings that make the headlines and are fun to read about.

The grandeur of the newly restored Waldorf-Astoria Ballroom: the tables are set for a lavish reception.

Nevertheless, most couples and their families want to go all out for this very special occasion—as far out as their bank accounts will permit. Sharing the wedding costs, once unheard of, is a happy solution. In Spain it has long been the custom for the father of the bride and the father of the groom to issue the invitations and co-host the wedding. Lately that sensible point of view has reached our shores. A *New York Times* article in 1980 told of a Long Island caterer who "re-

In Father of the Bride *Spencer Tracy has not only lost a daughter, he has gained a mountain of bills.*

ports that only a third of all reception expenses he handles are paid totally by the bride's parents. Of the remainder, one-third are split between the parents, and another third are paid, at least partially, by the bride and groom themselves."

Today's bride is older—frequently in her late twenties or thirties—with a mind, and often a salary, of her own. Her wedding is a celebration for both families, but especially for her! Hence the trend toward the bride-to-be paying a share of the expenses.

How do families split costs? Usually the bridegroom and his parents will pay for one or more of the major items: flowers, liquor, music. Or one family pays all ceremony-related costs while the other takes care of the reception. Often the couple themselves share in the final accounting, putting a down payment, as it were, on the new family they are creating.

Contrast this present liberalized view with former attitudes as expressed in this 1930s etiquette book and you can see how truly sympathetic our society has become to the father of the bride!

No matter what the means of the groom or his willingness to render financial aid, it is a hard and fast rule that the wedding must be given by the bride's family or by the bride herself, if she has no immediate relatives. The groom's mother may give a large reception for her son and his bride as soon as she likes after the wedding day, but not on the wedding day.

(Anna Steese, *The Bride's Book of Etiquette*)

Wedding Costs

Bride's gown	$426
Bride's veil	104
Invitations, announcements, thank-yous, etc.	200
Bouquets and other flowers	324
Photography	470
Music	369
Clergy, rabbi, church, chapel, synagogue fees	83
Limousine	58
Attendant gifts (bride's and groom's)	149
Wedding ring(s)	808
Mother of the bride's apparel	121
Bridal attendants' apparel	319
Men's formalwear	230
Groom's attire	55
Rehearsal dinner	293
Reception	2,000
TOTAL COST	$6,009

The above figures are those that have been documented by *Bride's* recently. The reception figure is the one most subject to variation. The style of the reception—whether just cake and champagne or a seated dinner with dancing—can influence the total tremendously, and up or down. What's more, costs differ depending on the region of the country. It is therefore very difficult to establish a single average figure; a range of $2,000–$4,000 for a wedding with a guest list of about 200 is probably close. This figure is based on an average expense of $10 per guest.

Next we will act, how young men wooe;
And sigh, and kiss, as Lovers do:
And talke of Brides; and who shall make
That wedding-smock, this Bridal-Cake;
That Dress, this Sprig, that Leaf, this Vine;
That smooth and silken Columbine.
This done, we'l draw lots, who shall buy
And guild the Baies and Rosemary:
What Posies for our Wedding Rings;
What Gloves we'll give, and Ribanings.

Robert Herrick

"The Honour of Your Presence . . ."

In 1969 George Gorner and Pamela Klein decided that it wouldn't be a proper wedding unless the whole world was invited, and they asked friends to help pass out their handmade invitations on the street. Some three hundred people showed up at their outdoor wedding in San Francisco's Golden Gate Park, two hundred of them strangers. Other weddings in the late sixties and early seventies took this communal spirit one step further when bride, groom, and attendants led a procession through the streets and, in the manner

A Country Wedding, *1951, Grandma Moses*

of the Middle Ages, welcomed bystanders to join the festivities.

There is an ancient instinct to include the surrounding world in wedding festivities, but this is often tempered by limitations: money, space, love of privacy. Most couples today choose to have a festive celebration, with their individual touches, to which they invite family and friends—one that is both traditional and very personal.

The diversity of today's households has led to a welcome creativity in wedding invitations. No longer are the couple and their parents bound by immutable laws of etiquette: divorced parents join

to issue an invitation to their daughter's wedding; a young couple may host their own celebration; adult children give away their remarrying parents. Even for formal invitations there are now no fewer than nine acceptable wordings, according to contemporary guides. And the variations for informal invitations are endless.

Wedding invitations reflect the bride and bridegroom's personal taste. Many still choose the most traditional style, which dates from the turn of the century—a black engraved script lettering on heavy cream paper. These classics imitate earlier handwritten invitations. A much less expen-

Mr. Douglas Wainwright
has the honour of announcing
the marriage of his daughter
Adelaide
to
Mr. Emerson Pearce Barton
on Saturday, the first of November
Nineteen hundred and seventy-five
Great Harbour Cay
The Bahamas

cation "Within the ribbon," which directs the guest to the seats near the front of the church reserved for close relatives and special friends. Travel arrangements and other last-minute instructions (what to do in case of rain) may also be included. Depending on the style of the invitation and the nature of the information, enclosures can be engraved, printed, handwritten, or photocopied (a method often used for maps).

Sometimes response cards are enclosed, for the recipient to fill in and mail back in place of a written answer, but the use of them is controversial. Until recently they were considered some-

Mr. and Mrs. Alfonso Williamson, 3rd
request the pleasure of your company
at the marriage of their daughter
Valerie
to
Mr. Paul Quincy Adams
on Sunday, the twenty-eighth of April
at half after four o'clock
Glen Oak Country Club
Chestnut Hill, Pennsylvania

R.s.v.p.
1200 Pine Street

sive process called thermography can produce results similar to engraving. There are also many other alternatives. Some invitations combine text (invitation, poems, and other personal messages) with photographs and drawings—of the couple, their parents, favorite flowers, even the wedding site.

If a bride chooses to have a large reception but invites only a limited number to the ceremony, she may send invitations to the reception and enclose ceremony cards in some of them. Customarily, enclosures signal a welcome to the reception, notice of the bride and groom's new address, or—in very formal weddings—the indi-

what commercial and déclassé. They do, however, eliminate the necessity of follow-up telephone calls for a busy bride and her family.

Wedding invitations offer guests their first sense of the tone and style of the coming event. And when they are beautifully designed and addressed, they are a lasting memento of this always unique celebration.

"Getting to Know You . . ."

Most couples today want to savor their engagement, a pause when their lives are on hold and they can plan not only for their long-dreamed-of wedding day, but also for their future life together. This freedom has as many responsibilities as it has rights. Implicit today is an obligation to use this time to truly explore the depth and breadth of the other person, to determine how each will react to the pressures of the years ahead, how seriously each will take the vows they will articulate at the altar. The goal is to reduce the divorce rate and stabilize the family structure. And there is a strong desire on the part of every engaged couple to work toward this goal—both before and after the marriage.

Today, preparing for marriage has become an art, and marriage a life's work. Education begins early, in high school and college, with family relations courses. Engaged couples receive counseling from the clergy, many of whom will not consider marrying them until after at least one or two lengthy meetings. They can enroll in groups like Engaged Encounter, which specialize in teaching the most basic communication techniques to couples who may be deeply in love, yet surprisingly unable to talk to each other.

MR. AND MRS. DUNCAN LAURENS FRANK

REQUEST THE HONOUR OF YOUR PRESENCE

AT THE MARRIAGE OF THEIR DAUGHTER

BARBARA

TO

MR. LYMAN ROBERT STRAUS

ON SATURDAY, THE TWENTIETH OF JUNE

AT HALF AFTER FOUR O'CLOCK

TEMPLE EMANU-EL

AND AT THE RECEPTION

FOLLOWING THE CEREMONY

1040 FIFTH AVENUE

NEW YORK

THE FAVOUR OF A REPLY IS REQUESTED

The honour of your presence
is requested at the marriage ceremony
at half after four o'clock
in the Chapel of
The Madison Avenue Presbyterian Church
New York

The amusing interaction between the man and woman in this tongue-in-cheek chronology of marriage is surprisingly liberal, for its time, in its presentation of the social power of women.

Marriage as Contract

What Jacqueline Kennedy Onassis had in common with many royal brides of the past was the fact that her marriage to Aristotle Onassis included a prenuptial contract. According to the *New York Times*, the legal papers, purportedly containing some 170 clauses, guaranteed her a lavish lifestyle, regardless of marital love and devotion, or even fidelity.

Prenuptial contracts are now permitted in over fifty percent of the states, usually as a result of the passage of equitable-distribution divorce laws. As New York City attorney Martin Kramer says,

OPPOSITE *While a long engagement like the one portrayed in this mid-nineteenth-century work may seem endless, modern couples find the time a valuable opportunity to test the seriousness of their devotion.*

"Contracts are not always important to the couple themselves, but are very helpful in protecting children and grandchildren."

Particularly valuable to the parent of a dependent child or for persons who are marrying for a second time, they are not a remedy for all possible problems. Depending on the laws of the state involved, a marriage contract might not only provide for the care and custody of the children and determine who gets what in case of a divorce or the death of one of the parties, but it might also provide for the terms of the marriage relationship. "A marriage contract allows the couple to define and limit or expand the obligations they want to take on," explains Ann Cynthia Diamond, another New York attorney. "The negotiation of such a contract can help a couple discover how each of them sees their life together developing, and gives them the opportunity to plan and to work out differences in advance."

Whether a couple decides to draw up a contract or not, the minimum prenuptial essentials—with a few exceptions—are still the marriage license and the blood test. Marriage vows perform the next indispensable legal function. When the bride says, "I, Mary, take thee, John," she is making a public pronouncement that she indeed wishes to marry, and to marry this particular partner. The wedding ceremony would be invalid without this statement.

The Marriage Contract

"ARTICLE 3: TERMS OF ENDEARMENT . . ."

Some brides today are bringing the signing of the marriage license out from behind closed doors. Following the exchange of rings and vows, the newly united pair, their honor attendants, and the officiant move to the side of the altar and sign the document in the presence of the congregation. Sometimes a special voice or instrumental solo accompanies this interlude. This is a sensitive way to combine the legal necessities with the joy and solemnity of the marriage sacrament.

Marriage is a status fixed by law. It differs from other legal contracts in the United States in that the husband and wife cannot just decide mutually to dissolve it. They must go through the legal procedure known as divorce which, like the marriage, requires a formal piece of paper.

American laws governing marriage are based on English common law, which regards husband and wife as one person, with the woman the one to surrender her property and identity. Until recently, a bride was required to change her surname to that of her husband, to live where her husband chose, even to give over her earnings to him. The husband, in turn, had a responsibility to support his wife as well as to compensate for any debts she incurred or crimes she committed.

Laws in every state change almost from day to day. In general, legislatures are relaxing restrictions and equalizing the statutes in favor of women. The movement toward humanization of the laws is strong, although some ridiculous ones governing marriage remained on the books until very recently. These may still be in effect:

- A married couple in Michigan must live together or be imprisoned.
- In Kentucky, a wife must have her husband's permission to move the furniture in her house.
- A judge in Michigan decided that a woman's hair is the property of her husband.
- In Minnesota, a hug and a kiss in the presence of a girl's parents, combined with several gifts of candy, is considered a proposal of marriage.

Pre-Wedding Jitters

Ghosts and demons portending all the possible disasters haunt the minds of the affianced in spite of their new maturity, their confidence in each other, and the liberated society in which we live. In arranged marriages there was often much to worry about, of course, since the bride and groom did not know one another. Not knowing how a husband-to-be will turn out can prove hazardous to the bride, as the story of Bluebeard illustrates. But today, at least in this country, friendship usually precedes marriage. Nevertheless, the average bride finds that with the stress of the wedding preparations, fears begin to nibble at her resolve.

It's quite normal to be nervous before your wedding, marriage counselors now agree. Among those questions that whirl about in every bride's mind are:

- Will I lose my privacy or hard-won independence after I marry?
- Will I lose my financial freedom?
- I was in love before, and it ended. Will that happen again?
- Does getting married mean becoming totally separate from my family?
- My fiancé and I have been fighting more since our engagement was announced. Is anything wrong?
- I'm really looking forward to our wedding night —so why am I so anxious?
- I want my wedding to be perfect. What if something goes wrong?

The most important thing family and friends can do is to reassure . . . reassure and set an example of calmness. Some degree of jitters is probably unavoidable—for the groom as well as the bride—but they'll evaporate as soon as the newlyweds head up the aisle together, arm in arm, husband and wife.

Pre-Wedding Parties

Pre-wedding gatherings are a traditional, exciting, integral part of the marriage celebration.

Over the years the bridal shower has given women a chance to share their good wishes with the bride.

Showers Wedding showers first began when friends, even entire communities, gathered to "stake" a young woman whose modest means might have been an impediment to marriage. The practice began in Holland, when a young girl's father disapproved of her beloved and refused to give her a dowry; the villagers banded together and "showered" her with everything needed for a new home. Another wedding custom, popular in the 1890s, involved putting presents into a brightly colored Japanese paper umbrella; when the bride popped it open over her head, the parcels "showered" down on her.

Thirty years ago showers were given for women only, trousseau and kitchen showers being among the most popular. Now, however, these happy occasions are often coed and might be based on themes such as wine and bar accessories, household equipment of all sorts, or gifts for sports enthusiasts. Expensive items are not the goal; it's the thought (and charm) that counts.

Bachelor dinner The bachelor party is steeped in tradition. Whether it is held at an elegant men's club, local watering place, or private home, the main activities are drinking and commiserating. Traditionally the purpose of the bachelor party was to raise a special fund for the groom so he could continue to drink with his buddies after his bride took control of the household finances. But mainly the bibulous camaraderie was a way of mourning the passing of one man's bachelor status. The bachelors were good sports, though. At some point, the group switched to champagne, and with great ceremony they toasted the bride. So they might never be used "for a less worthy purpose," the glasses were then smashed in a nearby fireplace, or lacking that, they were stamped underfoot.

Bachelor parties today are often quieter gatherings, a reunion of the groom's old friends, bachelors and otherwise, to reminisce and wish him well.

Bridesmaids' tea   At a traditional tea the bride presents her maids with thank-you gifts and serves them a special cake into which a ring has been baked. The bridesmaid who receives the lucky slice will be the next to marry.

With silk and lace lingerie so fashionable nowadays, brides are going back to showing off their negligees and other intimate finery at a trousseau tea—but never by modeling them, since it's considered bad luck to try these garments on before the wedding.

Another way for the bride to thank her bridesmaids is at a luncheon, often also attended by the mothers of the bride and groom. (For ideas about gifts for bridesmaids, see the following chapter.)

Some "liberated" brides imitate the bachelor party with some racy revelry of their own—a trip to the casinos, or a self-indulgent day at a spa.

Rehearsal dinner   The noisier the better was once the rule for parties that were held on the wedding eve—in order to chase away evil spirits. Glasses and plates were smashed in the melee, which lasted well into the night. Today's rehearsal dinner is far more subdued. Traditionally it is hosted by the bridegroom's parents to show generosity and hospitality to the bride's family (who are paying for the wedding). Sometimes this prenuptial dinner may be a large joint effort that includes out-of-town guests who've arrived early, and sometimes it is just a small intimate gathering of the wedding party and close friends—in either case it takes place after the bridesmaids and groomsmen have walked through their parts in the rehearsal for the next day's ceremony. (Superstition has it that the bride must only watch the rehearsal, often with a friend taking her role.)

When Princess May and the Duke of York married in 1893, their 3,500 wedding presents on view at Marlborough House made a staggering display. Think of the thank-you notes!

4
Wedding Gifts

The custom of giving presents to the bride and her groom is no doubt rooted in the human spirit of generosity. But there were practical concerns as well: wedding gifts are an outgrowth of the bride-price and dowry. Whether lavish or modest, they are symbols celebrating the couple's new life.

Here are some traditional wedding gifts from around the world:

• English brides received brass warming pans inscribed "Love and Live in Peace"; Austrian girls were given wooden tubs with "Be Happy and Industrious" painted on the side. They carried possessions to their new homes in the tubs.

• A pig has long been a traditional wedding gift in Herefordshire, England. As recently as 1910, a local blacksmith's daughter who had an otherwise formal wedding still received a pig from her father. But later she praised his gift as one of the most valuable: the pig produced twenty-eight piglets within a year!

• In Japan, the bridegroom gives the bride a bucket of clams and she makes a broth from it, which they drink together. At the betrothal party, the bridegroom's family gives the bride her wedding kimono, embroidered with the groom's crest. Then she receives a dress kimono, silk, shoes, hair ornaments, various foods—all in even-numbered amounts (two measures of tea, two pairs of toe thongs). Her family reciprocates with the identical presents for the groom, down to the number of fish packed as a picnic for the return to the bridegroom's house.

• In American colonial days, handcrafted items were popular, such as the embroidered samplers and quilts that were made by women in the community.

• Among Iroquois Indians, the bride and her mother brought maize cakes to the future mother-in-law's home; she gave them venison in return. This exchange of bread and meat was considered a marriage ceremony in itself.

• Finnish brides, until about a century ago, collected their wedding gifts in a comical procession from house to house. An old married man, wearing a top hat and carrying an umbrella to symbolize his sheltering role, accompanied the bride. At each house she stuffed her gifts into a pillowcase, while her protector was given a bit of intoxicating drink. By the end of the evening they made quite a pair—she burdened with a sack of goods, he rumpled and staggering from a night of drinking. Yet to eliminate this custom would have been considered snobbish.

• In Yorkshire, England, a girl marrying a farmer received a new "butter penney," which was balanced on a scale against a "pundstan," a stone weighing exactly one pound. The tradition ensured that no customer at the farm could complain of unfairness in transactions involving weight.

And finally, even though the bride has given her fiancé her heart, she still wants to give him some tangible possession that symbolizes her love. Traditionally she might give him something monogrammed, usually in gold or silver—something that will "last a lifetime." Or the bride may choose a gift that reflects her fiancé's personality—season tickets to sporting events, a camera lens, a tennis racket, flying lessons, a silk bathrobe, even a silver moustache comb!

The groom, too, may choose to give the bride something special to mark the day. A piece of fine jewelry, a watch, a piece of furniture, a beautiful picture frame or a desk accessory for her

ABOVE *This classic sterling silver bowl from Tiffany & Co. is a reproduction of a design by Jacob Hurd, Boston, 1702–58.*
BELOW *The goose and gander are a faithful couple, often given in pairs as wedding gifts in China. Eros rode on a goose, and wild geese are a symbol of ecstasy. This Steuben goose and gander, each formed of a single gather of crystal, have become a popular wedding gift in the United States.*

office are all appropriate. To add extra meaning he usually has his gift engraved with the wedding date or a sentimental phrase.

The Wedding Gift Registry

Publicizing wedding gifts was a popular custom in Edwardian England, when lists of presents and their donors were splashed across the pages of newspapers.

While listing wedding gifts in a newspaper seems crass to some people, it served the purpose of helping those guests who hadn't chosen their gifts to avoid duplications and to select something that would fit in with the bride's other possessions. Today we have the wedding gift registry to guide us.

As far as we know, the first wedding gift registry appeared in 1901 in a store called China Hall in Rochester, Minnesota. A young clerk, Herman Winkle, couldn't remember the gifts various brides had received when shoppers asked him for assistance, so he began to write down the brides' names on index cards with lists of gifts they had already received and patterns they had chosen.

According to Richard Winkle (Herman's son), popular wedding gifts around the turn of the century were hand-painted and hand-cut glass and crystal, glass berry sets, hand-painted serving dishes, butter churns, parlor lamps, and vases. Dinnerware and stemware were not commonly given by wedding guests because they could be purchased only in full sets—at that time a full set was 90 to 200 pieces!

Wedding gift registries became widely popular in jewelry stores in the mid-1930s and were soon adopted by department stores, and more recently

• Princess May and the Duke of York upon their marriage in 1893 received more than 3,500 gifts. Among these were a diamond and pearl necklace from the "Ladies of England," a diamond and pearl comb, and a spray of foliage in diamonds. The King presented the bride with a festoon of pearls—520 in all—and a diamond brooch and rose.

• Princess Marina and Prince George were given a set of sapphires and diamonds by Prince George's mother for their wedding in 1934, as well as a necklace of 372 historic family pearls punctuated with diamond motifs.

• President Grant's daughter Nellie received some $75,000 worth of gifts at her marriage to Algernon Charles Frederick Satoris in 1874, including a $500 handkerchief.

• When Alice Roosevelt, daughter of President Theodore, married Congressman Nicholas Longworth in 1906, the president of France sent a $25,000 Gobelin tapestry and the Pope gave the couple a mosaic table. A $1,500 Boston terrier arrived complete with an engraved silver schedule of the dog's daily routine and a wardrobe of canine suits and costumes. The government of Cuba gave the bride a $30,000 pearl necklace, while the city of Cincinnati sent a team of matched horses. One gift, a punch bowl from the Ohio delegation, so upset the Women's Christian Temperance Union that Congress got involved in the fuss and a loving cup was finally substituted.

• In addition to the many splendid and extravagant gifts that Princess Diana received were some that may not have cost much but were rich in sentiment: a needle case, a decorated egg, a set of felt mice, a bookmark, pottery mugs, a picture composed of pressed flowers—all made by their donors.

• One of Luci Johnson's favorite gifts was a jeweled Pakistani nose ring, symbolizing female submission, given by Orville Freeman, her father's secretary of agriculture.

ABOVE *"Honfleur" is one of the most popular china patterns with registered brides.*
BELOW *This sterling silver "barrel bowl" was adapted from an eighteenth-century English design.*

Celeste Holm and Frank Sinatra sing delightedly about the wealth of wedding gifts in the 1956 version of Philadelphia Story.

by furniture stores and gourmet shops. Now wedding gift registries, often computerized, can be found at a variety of places: book stores, liquor stores, and many kinds of specialty shops. A few years ago, the Metropolitan Museum of Art in New York City started a wedding gift registry where couples could list items such as art prints and reproductions of the museum's antique porcelain, silver, and glassware, as well as copies of many of the artworks on display there.

When wedding guests go to a wedding gift registry, the consultant shows them what the bride and bridegroom have chosen. As soon as guests purchase an item, it's checked off the list to avoid duplication. Guests can use the registry to select a specific gift, or as a general guideline to the bride's taste.

Money as a Gift

There is one popular wedding gift that can't be registered for: money. Wedding gifts of money have been traditional since the days of bride-price and dowry, when cash (in whatever form that culture used) was exchanged during betrothal negotiations. Couples in many cultures have appreciated monetary gifts ever since.

Guests slip money to brides in a number of charming ways favored by custom. The Chinese put their gift of cash in a special red envelope (red is the Chinese color of good luck), decorated with symbols wishing the couple a long life together. In Eastern European countries it is a centuries-old tradition for male wedding guests to pay for the honor of dancing with the bride. Polish guests pin bills to the bride's dress, a rather difficult proposition; in other countries the bride may wear an apron with pockets to collect the money. Or she can place it in a decorative bag of silk or satin, perhaps trimmed with lace, ribbons, or beads.

Finnish brides used to collect their wedding gift money in a sieve held on their lap. As guests placed their donations in the sieve, an usher called out their name and the amount of the donation. In Russia and Japan, when guests give money, they receive a small present from the couple in exchange.

For the Attendants

"Gifts for the attendants haven't changed much over the years," says Ralph Destino, president of Cartier in New York. "Brides look for small, personal items: jewelry, pens, picture frames. A great favorite for ushers are silver julep cups. If a man has been an usher often, he can start a set."

Listed below are some of the most popular gifts a bride and groom can choose to thank the friends and family who have played supporting roles at their wedding. The rehearsal is a nice time to honor these people with a gift and a special word of thanks.

For bridesmaids and best women: bracelets, charms for bracelets, small vases, key rings, boxes (china, porcelain, ceramic, wooden), necklaces, the dresses they wear at the wedding, framed wedding photographs, earrings, stickpins, lockets, silk flowers, evening bags, hair ornaments, monogrammed stationery, perfume bottles.

For ushers and best men: mugs (silver, pewter, ceramic), cuff links, tie tacks, watches, calculators, key chains, manicure kits, tickets to sport-

A charming table setting for a bridal party: at each place is a gift from the bride to her attendants.

ing events, books, money clips, pens, pocket knives, letter openers, bar glasses and accessories, clocks, grooming kits, imprinted notepads.

For children: drawing pads with pens or crayons, craft kits; coins, stamps, or other collectibles; balls, jewelry, dolls, piggy banks, mugs.

For parents: silver picture frames, toasting glasses, lace or embroidered tablecloths, clocks, gift certificates, trays, scrapbooks, engraved plaques and paperweights, serving spoons, vases.

5
The Ceremony

ere Comes the Bride . . ." The first strains of the wedding music signal the beginning of a processional that is rooted in dance; dancing is an essential element of celebration, emphasizing as it does the energy of life. Courtship is a private pas de deux between a man and a woman as they decide whether or not to marry. Engagement is more of a square dance—a patterned working out of the details of a merger between families. But weddings—ah, weddings! They have a way of gathering all the world into the procession. A wedding is a courtly pavane, one in which all generations can participate as the bride and groom weave back through history and forward into the unchoreographed future.

And so there is a shared feeling of expectation at that thrilling moment when the first chord is sounded. A communal joy transcends the gravity of the occasion as the congregation—the families and friends—rise to view the bride in her marriage procession.

An Italian groom on his wedding day used to proceed with family and friends to the bride's house, where his father would claim the bride and the guests would shower her with wheat, bread, and salt—symbols of fertility and plenty. Then both families would march together to the church for the actual marriage and blessing. Romanian brides walked to the church through their village, accompanied by flute players and violinists who issued wedding invitations in impromptu verse.

The Chinese frightened away evil spirits with a painting of a Taoist priest riding a tiger and carrying a sword. And in Manchuria, two men waved red cloths in front of the bridal procession. Evil spirits, it was thought, lived below the ground, so the bride whose feet never touched the ground would be safe. The red carpet and white aisle runner are vestiges of the many fanciful ways that brides were kept "walking on air."

In ancient times, the wedding torch—a symbol of life and love—was carried ahead of the bridal procession. The solemn ceremonies in Shakespeare's plays and the procession in the opera *Lucia di Lammermoor* act out this tradition, as the bride's way is lighted with torches and panoply. Today many brides ride or walk to the ceremony with as much fanfare as their forebears did, giving friends who cannot be invited to the actual ceremony a chance to wave, cheer, and show approval.

Wedding Music

The bridal chorus from *Lohengrin* ("Here Comes the Bride") was first played as a wedding processional in New York around 1860. The occasion was the wedding of an American heiress to a titled (but impoverished) European. Ward McAllister, a social leader of the day, suggested the piece after hearing Wagner's opera in Germany. Nineteenth-century America was still newly rich and musically unsure of itself; anything by Wagner seemed to have the right touch of continental class.

Although the opera itself ends unhappily, *Lohengrin* was stamped with royal approval when Princess Louise of England selected it for her wedding in 1899. In fact, royal weddings continue to inspire brides today: the "Trumpet Voluntary in D Major" by Jeremiah Clarke, also

OPPOSITE *A traditional Japanese bridal gown and headdress.*

An old-fashioned European village wedding is enlivened by the music of a violin.

known as the "Prince of Denmark's March," has become a new bridal classic since it was played at the wedding of Prince Charles and Lady Diana Spencer in 1981.

Many other selections are popular with brides who search through music from the Renaissance to the present for inspiration: "Jesu, Joy of Man's Desiring" by Johann Sebastian Bach; "Trumpet Tune" by Henry Purcell; a rigaudon by André Campra, a French contemporary of Bach's; "Coronation March" by Sir William Walton; "Marche Romaine" by Charles Gounod; "Sortie" by César Franck; "Psalm 19" by Benedetto Marcello; "Water Music" by George Frederick Handel; "Adagio" by Tomaso Albinoni; and almost any of the English madrigals number among the current favorites.

Couples today tend to choose the more serious

festive music for a religious ceremony. This respect for tradition with an accent on personal style has also swept Johann Pachelbel's "Canon in D" into prominence for its mystical and lyrical connotations. But there are sounds for every soul —from jungle drums to love songs. Devout churchgoers frown, believing even Wagner to be too secular for a truly religious service.

The ritual dance continues after the vows are said. The recessional classic, Mendelssohn's "Wedding March" from "A Midsummer Night's Dream," or another joyous selection signals the new status of the bride as she and her husband leave in a shower of rice and good wishes.

OPPOSITE *The processional begins, in a dream setting that calls for Handel or Bach.*

BEATON

GEENE GLENNY

All Brides Are Beautiful

A bride is described as a "vision of beauty" and her gown as "heavenly," as though she were, in fact, angelic. Indeed, in rowdier times past, belief in the mystical value of her adornments prompted friends and strangers alike to try to wrest an enchanted piece of lace or ribbon from her dress for

Lace: The Ultimate Bridal Finery

Laces, intricate openwork so fine and delicate that it might take months to make a square inch, were rightly regarded as fine art in Europe. Venice was the lacemaking capital of the world, although England, Belgium, and France were justifiably proud of the exquisite handiwork of their artisans. These laces were sewn on dresses, veils, and gloves so everyone could appreciate their charm and grace, and when delicate underpinnings were frothed with lace, a stolen glimpse of frilly hem was a delightful treat. Rare as it was for her, many a peasant bride sewed just a bit of the fragile stuff, usually homemade, on her ceremonial apron. A fragile lace handkerchief carried by the bride may be an heirloom already, or surely will be one for future generations.

their own good-luck charm. Now, however, they content themselves with catching her garter or bouquet.

The bride has succeeded in remaining noble and adored in song and story—whether dressed in animal skins or Alençon lace. Her elegance comes not so much from what she wears, although there have been wedding dresses that rival the most sumptuous of royal robes. Rather it is her bearing, the unmistakable aura that surrounds her in her progress through this rite of passage. And there is her sense of presence—the transfiguration that occurs the moment the organ sounds. The feeling is captured beautifully in John Gardner's *Nickel Mountain*. The bride, Cal-

The paper-doll bride is make-believe magic.

purer, immutable as the gown was not, as even the ceremony was not. Their faces surrounded her, looking up, shining as if reflecting the secret radiance thinly veiled, her total and untouchable, virginal freedom. In a moment, she would feel her weight again, her mere humanness, the child inside, but not yet. The church window said, *All will be well.*

The Bridal Gown Traditionally, ceremonial robes have often been richly colored, whether they were peasant costumes or gold-embroidered kimonos, and in many cases they were handed down from generation to generation. During the Middle Ages, for instance, red was the favored color, and it is still the color chosen by Hindu, Islamic, and Chinese brides as a symbol of celebration. This "color of defiance" was also worn by brides during the American Revolution. In Iceland, on the other hand, black velvet embroidered with gold and silver thread was the fashion as recently as fifty years ago.

The white wedding dress, so much a part of our romantic vision today, is a fairly recent tradition. Victorian brides from privileged backgrounds wore white to indicate that they were rich enough to wear a dress for one day only—but still the majority at that time simply wore their best finery. Even when white had caught on as a symbol of purity, the dresses were often worn more than once. At the turn of the century, women wore their wedding dresses on special occasions throughout the first year of their marriage. And today a bride might shorten or restyle her wedding gown, to keep it as a sentimental favorite in her wardrobe. But the majority of brides now put the treasured dress away, preserved as a memento

lie, does not feel attractive, isn't terribly excited about this marriage, and she's pregnant. And yet . . .

She walked slowly, having all eternity to taste the strange new sensation of freedom, knowing that she too was beautiful now, yet more beautiful than the wedding gown, lighter,

A French wedding gown, c. 1930, from the Brooklyn Museum.

or reserved for another bride in the family. The association of white with purity has relaxed, and these days the color symbolizes just the celebration itself. Indeed, many brides in America choose national dress reflecting their family's ethnic background in addition to their traditional white wedding dress. Like the Japanese, they often marry in one bridal costume, then change to another ethnic dress for the dancing. The bride of Polish descent, for example, dons an embroidered apron with huge pockets to catch the money gifts that are deposited during the wedding-party revelry.

This bridal headdress of kingfisher feathers and metal graced the brow of a Chinese bride long ago.

Married in white, you have chosen all right;
Married in grey, you will go far away;
Married in black, you will wish yourself back;
Married in red, you wish yourself dead;
Married in green, ashamed to be seen;
Married in blue, he will always be true;
Married in pearl, you will live in a whirl;
Married in yellow, ashamed of your fellow;
Married in brown, you will live out of town;
Married in pink, your fortune will sink.

Anonymous Victorian verse

The Wedding Veil   The veil, one of the most ancient of wedding traditions, has always stood for youth and virginity. In some Moslem countries where a woman may not show her face, the innocent bride is veiled all during the wedding ceremony. This curtain of mystery is dropped only before her husband and at the family wedding feast.

In the United States, the veil was not part of a colonial wedding costume. When the widow Martha Custis was married to a resplendent George Washington in 1759, she wore a gown of white satin and diamond-buckled shoes—but no veil.

Old Afghan customs include zaraq, *the complicated art of adorning the bride for the ceremony.*

But Martha Custis's "daughter," Nellie, an incurable romantic, inadvertently set a trend. She was sitting by a lace-curtained window when her stepfather's aide, Lawrence Lewis, walked by and saw her lace-framed face. It was love at first sight and clever Nellie later re-created the flattering effect by wearing lacy veiling when she married Lawrence.

The Headpiece This term is applied to a number of bridal headcoverings—from lace mantillas and garlands to hats—which have evolved over the centuries. Swathes of brilliant yellow that "shielded the downcast looks of virgin modesty" were the Roman choice. The Viking queens wore metal skullcaps. Japanese brides still wear the traditional "tsuno-kakushi," a white hood that supposedly hides the horns of jealousy.

In this century, bridal hats came into fashion.

They blossom like garden flowers in the summer months when outdoor weddings are at their prettiest and most romantic.

The Wedding Crown The Archbishop of Canterbury pronounced these words during the marriage of Prince Charles and Lady Diana Spencer on July 29, 1981:

There is an ancient Christian tradition that every bride and groom on their wedding day are regarded as a royal couple. To this day, in the marriage ceremonies of the Eastern Orthodox Church, crowns are held over the man and the woman to express the conviction that as husband and wife, they are kings and queens of creation. As it says of humankind in the Bible, "Thou crownedst him with glory and honor, and didst set him over the work of Thy hands."

The traditional crowns were held over the heads of this couple, married in a Russian Orthodox ceremony in London.

The symbolic wedding crown can vary from a simple one of flowers to the elaborate headdress that Japanese brides wear to this day—so heavy that they often have to be aided as they move to their groom's side.

But the more familiar headpiece and veil symbolize for the rest of us the bride's majesty, as on her special day she dresses in royal "robes," rides in a coach—even if it is only the shiniest car in the neighborhood—and presides at a feast. And we all wish on her star for a life that will be happy forever after.

The Train The train is an extension of the presence of the bride, leaving an aura of grandeur in her wake. Royal women, often trying to outdo one another in splendor, have worn "endless" trains woven with silver and gold thread, trimmed in pearls and diamonds, and edged in ermine and other furs. H.R.H. Princess Elizabeth chose to march down the aisle with a fifteen-foot court train of ivory silk tulle; Lady Diana Spencer commissioned a twenty-five-foot silken sweep.

Trains today are still extremely popular, but although many romantic brides feel "the longer, the better," they are often modified for practicality's sake. The sweep (just touching the floor), chapel (trailing along behind), and cathedral train (over three feet long) are the ones most often chosen.

The splendor and pageantry of czarist Russia is reflected in this old engraving.
Every bride and groom begins wedded life as royalty.
The candles in the couple's hands represent the spiritual lifting of a prayer to God.

Flowers

For generations of brides, the romantic touch of rose petals, the sight of lighthearted tulips, the spicy aroma of carnations, have stirred the senses and spoken of love. Flowers are synonymous with

Flowers and Their Meanings

Acacia – Friendship

Anemone – Anticipation

White Carnation – "Remember me"

Crocus – Joy

Forget-me-not – True love

Holly – Domestic happiness

Honeysuckle – Faithfulness

Ivy – Fidelity

Purple lilac – First love

White lilac – Innocence

Lily-of-the-valley – Purity

Orange Blossom – Fertility, happiness

Orchid – "You are beautiful"

Red rose – "I love you"

White rose – "You're heavenly"

Red and white roses together – Unity

Sage – Domestic virtue

Snowdrop – Friendship, purity

Sweet William – "Smile for me"

Violet – Modesty

Water lily – A pure heart

Zinnia – Thoughts of friends

virginity, femininity, fragility. And the bridal bouquet—whether traditionally all white or in colors as radiant as a stained-glass window—brings a time-honored custom to the wedding day.

The first bouquets carried by brides consisted not of blossoms but of herbs, whose strong aromas were believed to ward off evil spirits. Rosemary had the added gift of ensuring remembrance, and a sprig from the bouquet, along with other herbs such as dill (which "provoked lust"), was often eaten for its alleged powers. Marigolds, gilded and dipped in fragrant rosewater, were also eaten by brides in Tudor England for their presumed aphrodisiac effect.

In a wedding sermon given in 1607, Reverend Roger Hackett said, "Let this Ros Marinus—the flower of men, ensigne of your wisdome, love and loyaltie—be carried, not only in your hands, but in your heads and hearts." Through the ages flowers, like herbs, have become symbolic of various qualities. Medieval brides wore garlands of fresh blossoms in their hair, hoping to imbue their marriage with the flowers' attributes. Many a bride today wears her veil floating from a flowery wreath (though often made of silk replicas), quite unaware of its original significance.

Queen Victoria clutched a bridal nosegay of delicate snowdrops because they were her beloved

The Origin of the Bridal Wreath

Once upon a time, during the Dark Ages, orange trees were imported to Spain from the Orient at great expense . . . and were the property of the King.

The King's grove was tended by a gardener whose beautiful daughter wished to marry a very handsome, but penniless, young man. But the gardener forbade the union, and the maiden was very sad. Without a dowry she could do nothing.

Another gentleman, a young nobleman, who was forbidden to import his own orange trees, knew her proximity to the orange grove and came to ask if she could take just one little cutting for him to plant and nurture. He would pay her handsomely. She was sorely tempted. But her conscience worried her. Finally she went to the Queen, threw herself on her mercy, and asked for advice.

The Queen, who was very romantic herself, was so touched by the story that she presented the maiden with not only one of the young potted trees, but a royal blessing and a string of gold beads as a wedding gift.

And the young nobleman not only kept his promise, but gave her double the amount he had promised for this beautiful little tree.

She was now free to marry. While dressing for the ceremony, her eyes lighted upon a spray of orange blossoms upon the table. Quickly she twined it into the wreath that held her wedding veil.

The story spread through Spain and into the rest of Europe, and now every bride in the civilized world demands a wreath of orange blossoms and will wear no other.

Bride's Magazine, 1935

Albert's favorite flower. Princess Grace, after much thought, selected lilies-of-the-valley as the perfect complement to her regal gown (and no doubt she knew their meaning). And in 1968, when Jacqueline Kennedy and Aristotle Onassis were married, the couple were crowned with orange blossoms as they circled the altar in traditional Greek style.

Orange blossoms, the choice of many White House brides (such as Alice Roosevelt Longworth), have a long history as a wedding flower; it is said that Juno, Roman goddess of marriage,

Harry and Bess Truman on their wedding day, June 28, 1919.

gave these fragrant blossoms to Jupiter on their wedding day.

Flowers to decorate the site as well as the wedding party are selected for sentimental and even mystical reasons. If she wishes, a bride today can have almost any flower of her choosing regardless of the season—spring lilacs and hyacinths, the vivid anemones of summer, and the chrysanthemums and sheaves of wheat of autumn are available year round, arriving daily by air from flower markets in Europe and South America.

"With This Ring I Thee Wed"

Since primitive times, brides and bridegrooms have sealed the bargain with a symbolic exchange of rings. In song and story, in folklore and fantasy, once this exchange takes place the marriage begins. Circlets of rushes, which had to be renewed often, sufficed in early days, but when metals were discovered, their durability more fittingly typified the lasting quality of marriage.

Although it has been an object of superstition and reverence for centuries, a ring is not required to make a marriage valid under civil law in the United States. Rings were, however, declared an essential part of the marriage sacrament in the sixteenth century by the Council of Trent. Until then, Christian men had married by "spousals" —a simple statement of their intention. Puritan clergymen were displeased by the council's ruling, seeing in the wedding ring "a relique of popery and a diabolical circle for the devil to dance in." Yet Puritan men and women—not generally a rebellious group—continued to wear them anyway. In a few parts of the world, a marriage contract is still invalid without a gold ring.

Millions of couples exchange rings at their weddings. The tradition of "trust rings" *(trauringe)*, as the Germans called them, began in Roman times when a coin was given, half to the wife and half to the husband. (Was some creative lover inspired to beat his two half-coins into twin rings and thus start a whole industry?) Though the custom was almost universally honored in Europe, it took World War II to make the exchange of wedding rings a solid American tradition. Soldiers on their way overseas wanted to carry with them some token of home and wife,

Romantic traditions continue to proliferate as brides look back into history and to their ethnic origins. Some are time-honored——the custom of planting a flowering shrub or tree near the couple's new home, the Victorian way of arranging a bouquet to spell out the groom's name (baby's breath, irises, limonium, and lilies for B-I-L-L). Other purely personal customs are born each day. One couple left their ceremony under a shower of petals from all the roses he had sent her during their courtship, lovingly saved. Another bride took her groom's boutonnière from its place in her bouquet and pinned it on his lapel at the altar. In the language of love, flowers can say it all.

and in one year (1943), the number of double-ring ceremonies jumped from fifteen to eighty percent.

Now nearly ninety percent of couples who wed exchange rings. Men have very sentimental feelings about their rings; they view the ring as a symbol of love and support, see the giver of the ring as always near, or believe that the mutual exchange keeps love alive.

Many brides choose a heavy gold band or a more elaborate ring which combines several types of gold and is designed with dimensional surfaces or geometric planes. Others find an antique look more appealing, favoring the best Florentine workmanship in scrolled or etched gold, possibly accented with gemstones.

The pharaohs of Egypt wore their wedding ring on the third finger of the left hand because of the *vena amoris,* a vein which they believed ran from that finger directly to the heart. A pretty sentiment, but no X-ray has yet shown that such a vein exists. In many cultures the wedding ring is worn on another finger, but the pharaoh's finger remains the choice of most Americans.

To the ancients, the circular shape of the ring symbolized eternity; and even today, Orthodox Jews and other religious groups marry with rings that have no stones or other "interruptions" that might affect that heavenly circle in which life and happiness have no beginning and no end. Many brides refuse to ever remove their rings for fear of placing their marriage in jeopardy.

Talismans

When the bride chooses a talisman to take with her as she steps into the future, she still has one foot in the past. The custom of wearing something old, new, borrowed, and blue, as well as a good luck coin in the shoe, is rooted in the potent mix of tradition and superstition.

• Something old: A family heirloom—perhaps a Bible, antique lace sewn into the bridal gown, or a piece of jewelry—provides a sense of continuity.

• Something new: Most of the bride's clothes will be new, but special lingerie or some unaccustomed luxury adds an optimistic note.

• Something borrowed: There is a superstition that happiness rubs off. A lacy handkerchief or bit of jewelry borrowed from a happily married friend or relative is the choice of many brides.

• Something blue: Brides in Israel wear a blue ribbon, denoting purity, fidelity, and love. Blue is

"The Quakers have a beautiful tradition where the entire congregation, as witness, signs the wedding license," says Karen, a bride from Mt. Lebanon, Pennsylvania. "We decided to adapt this by having our vows hand-printed on parchment and, at the conclusion of the ceremony, inviting all our guests to sign our document." Today the license hangs above our fireplace, "a treasured reminder of the vows we pledged and a unique memento of all the family and friends who helped us celebrate our wedding."

The beauty of the bride doesn't stop with her veil and gown; it can be layers deep, with lace and ribbons hiding under the fullness of a ruffled skirt.

also associated with the Virgin Mary. Sometimes the bride has blue ribbon threaded through the lace of her slip, or on her garter.

• A penny in your shoe: In England a sixpence, in Canada a quarter, in the United States a penny —all help ensure a life of fortune.

Other customs include sewing into the hem of the bride's wedding petticoat a small pouch filled with a tiny piece of bread, a bit of cloth, a sliver of wood, and a dollar bill: to protect against future shortages of food, clothing, shelter, money. Brides in Greece believe a lump of sugar tucked into one of their wedding gloves will bring sweetness all their married lives. Lady Diana Spencer had a tiny silver horseshoe sewn into the waist-band of her dress. After the ceremony the Prince and Princess of Wales traveled to Buckingham Palace in a 1902 State Postillion Landau in which there was a full-sized version of the horse-shoe—in silver, of course!

"She Walks in Beauty"

As the bride dresses for her celebration, she may prepare in many different ways. Her attendants may bathe her in fragrant oils, as did the Romans, or like the Hindus may paint her hands and feet with henna. In Afghanistan, the exotic art of *zaraq* has been perfected over the centuries: the

bride's face is adorned with colored spangles and gilt paper strips, while in the manner of the Medici princesses, her hair is plucked high on her forehead. In many parts of Africa, as well as in America, ceremonial marriage headdresses often include numerous decorative braids.

In every country and throughout history, beauty rituals have exaggerated the features and the very image of the bride through makeup and hair arrangements as dramatic as they are colorful. Today the typical American bride glows with health and vitality on her wedding day. Her makeup is subtle yet effective, her hair shines, her body is toned. Although she may not, like privileged Indian brides of earlier times, be massaged with special oils every day for a month before her wedding, or like Arab women, have all her body hair removed, she will probably spend at least a few hours consulting a hairdresser and makeup artist, and perhaps have a facial or one-hour massage.

The modern bride's goal is healthy beauty: the radiance born of exercise, sound nourishment, and a positive attitude toward the future.

In general, mothers of the bride and groom wear pretty pastel dresses that harmonize with the entire wedding party. In the afternoon, they may be short, ankle or tea length. Evening weddings, especially when they are formal, call for long gowns, glamour and glitter.

The Grand (Male) Traditions

Raise high the rafters!
Hoist them higher!
Here comes the bridegroom,
taller than Ares,
Taller even than a tall man . . .
        (Sappho,
        "Hymen Hymenaon!")

As elegant as a man looks in evening clothes, he is even more impressive in the less familiar morning coat, or cutaway, designed in the last century

While the bride is glowing in her wedding finery, her groom traditionally appears in more sober clothing like this gray coat and pin-striped trousers.

When one's father is Governor of the Tower of London, the wedding party takes on special pageantry, with Beefeaters escorting the bride and her father to the church.

for semiformal occasions. In general, choices for the adventurous groom today are somewhat more subdued than they were during the 1960s when formal attire in apricot, yellow, and other pastel shades was all the rage. The wedding in which both the groom and his bride wear white remains somewhat popular in the United States. But there are those who rejoice in the return to convention.

The traditional male complement to the bride's finery is simply:

Formal daytime:	Gray trousers and stroller coat
Very formal daytime:	Gray trousers and cutaway
Formal evening:	Black tuxedo or dinner jacket
Very formal evening:	White tie and tails (top hat optional)

Also available are tuxedos and tails in a range of dark colors—burgundy, brown, navy—for contemporary formal weddings. These may be worn with similarly somber accoutrements or combined with more colorful ties, vests, and cummerbunds.

Dear bride, remember, if you can,

That thing you married is a man.

His thoughts are low, his mind is earthy,

Of you he is totally unworthy;

Wherein lies a lesson too few have larnt it—

That's the reason you married him, aren't it?

The organ booms, the procession begins,

The rejected suitors square their chins,

And angels swell the harmonious tide

Of blessings upon the bonnie bride.

But blessings also on him without whom

There would be no bride. I mean the groom.

*Ogden Nash, "Everybody Loves
a Bride, Even the Groom"*

Bridesmaids

A happy bridesmaid makes a happy bride.
(Alfred, Lord Tennyson)

Since brides of earlier times were often mere children, it was quite usual for them to be dressed for the occasion by someone older—and perhaps wiser. So much lore, so many charms developed out of the superstitions of those who hoped that this marriage, above all others, would be totally happy and fruitful.

The bride's siblings and maiden friends were often called upon to assist in these rituals. They prepared her costume and helped her dress, and in many cases aided in moving her worldly possessions to her next home. In fifth-century Britain, bridesmaids helped assemble the floral wreaths for all the members of the wedding. Now, in preparation for a large wedding, there are dozens of small chores that bridesmaids may discharge for a grateful bride.

But nowhere was the bridesmaids' assistance more vital to the bride than when they actually took her place in order to ward off evil spirits. This custom evolved out of pure fear, for it was believed that the bride and groom would be singled out for mischief, or worse, on their way to the church. It was important to protect them by confusing anyone who would do them harm. Group disguises, with bridesmaids and groomsmen indistinguishable from the happy couple, led to the fashion of identical dressing—hence the wedding party we know today with the bridesmaids in similar gowns. In Victorian times it was quite usual for the bridesmaids to be dressed all in white along with the bride, and some contemporary weddings still embrace this tradition. More popular, however, is the colorful contrast to the bride offered by pinks, lilacs, apricots, and yellows in the summer months, or the jewel colors—sapphire, emerald, tourmaline, garnet—at winter weddings.

The Best Woman The tradition of the best man is well entrenched. He is the one who straightens the groom's tie, gets him to the church on time, makes sure he has the ring, and

The bride and bridesmaids prepare for the ceremony—a special sorority sees the bride into her new role.

knows the right antidote for prenuptial jitters. The best man sees to it that the groom does not for a moment, though the spotlight is full on his bride, feel like the forgotten man.

Now there is a new idea: the best woman. This title is fondly bestowed upon the honor attendant who is married and dislikes the sound of "matron" or who is attending an older or remarrying bride. Naturally, if she is unmarried, she is still the maid of honor. She too keeps track of the ring, as well as holding the bride's bouquet.

The Wedding Service

There are endless possibilities for wedding liturgy, some centuries old, some the creation of the wedding couple. Although entire ceremonies were rewritten by couples experimenting with new forms in the 1960s, today they tend to make a more conservative choice. The selection of readings can personalize the service and offer an opportunity to involve family members and special friends in the ceremony.

Many couples choose the passionate lines from the Old Testament's "Song of Solomon," a celebration of faithful love reinterpreted by Christian theologians to represent the love between Christ (the bridegroom) and the Church (the bride).

My beloved spake, and said unto me,
Rise up, my love, my fair one, and come away.
For, lo, the winter is past, the rain is over and gone;
The flowers appear on the earth;
the time of the singing of birds is come,
and the voice of the turtle is heard in our land;
The fig tree putteth forth her green figs,

A wedding attended by noted feminist Gloria Steinem included this passage in the ceremony:

This is a wedding of two people, not two roles. Karin and Martin are here — not A Bride, not A Groom. Not one person and one possession. No one but no one — not even her family, not even we who are her sisters — can give Karin away. And no one can be given her. She belongs to herself.

and the vines with the tender grape give a good smell.
Arise, my love, my fair one, and come away.

* * *

Set me as a seal upon thine heart,
as a seal upon thine arm:
for love is strong as death;
jealousy is cruel as the grave:
the coals thereof are coals of fire,
which hath a most vehement flame.

The poetry of Robert Frost, George Eliot, and Elizabeth Barrett Browning provides popular romantic sayings, as do the lyrics of contemporary songwriters. But classic throughout this century have been the stirring words of the Indian poet Kahlil Gibran:

Let there be space in your togetherness
And let the winds of heaven dance between you.

The January 6, 1759, wedding of General George Washington to Martha Custis, to whom he "paid his address successfully," is depicted here with eighteenth-century elegance.

Love one another, but make not a bond of love;
Let it rather be a moving sea between the shores
*   of your souls,*
Fill each other's cup but drink not from one cup.
Give one another of your bread but eat not from
*   the same loaf.*
Sing and dance together and be joyous, but let
*   each one of you be alone,*
Even as the strings of a lute are alone though
*   they quiver with the same music.*

*   *   *   ***

Give your hearts, but not into each other's keeping.
For only the hand of Life can contain your hearts.
And stand together yet not too near together;

For the pillars of the temple stand apart,
And the oak tree and the cypress grow not in
*   each other's shadow.*

Today's bride marries by choice. The relationship of the bride to her father, and later to her husband, has shifted dramatically in recent years. Many a bride prefers to change the traditional "Who giveth this woman . . ." to words more indicative of her current status.

Although she is still escorted to the altar by one (Christian) or both (Jewish) parents, the feeling now is one of joining rather than giving the bride to the groom. Families and friends pledge

An old Hungarian marriage custom has bride and groom stand back-to-back
until their mothers clasp hands, indicating approval of the match.

to "support" the couple in their marriage. The blessing of the union takes precedence over the notion that the woman is being "transferred" from one role to another. And the couple go beyond mere civil law by reciting vows which may be both traditional and personal.

Contemporary clergy may emphasize the importance of this new beginning, then ask, "Who joins them in their happiness?" Both sets of parents, even the whole congregation, may answer "We do," and the couple's pledge of faith in the future can begin.

The Vows

"I do, I do."
How easily it's said.
I wonder what would happen
if I said "I don't" instead!
    (Tom Jones, *I Do! I Do!*)

Everyone strains forward as the hushed moment for the exchange of vows approaches. Once spoken, these solemn words of commitment affect the future not only of the couple themselves, but of their families, friends . . . and the community at large.

In some cultures, the bridegroom has never seen his bride until this moment, and even then he may be able to see only a mirror reflection of her image until their actual union is pronounced. Lady Diana Spencer nervously reversed her husband's names while Prince Charles (perhaps in chivalry?) confused his vows. Jane Eyre heard the incredible words of dissent from the back of the church as she stood before the altar with her beloved, Mr. Rochester. There is a natural, almost supernatural, tension that pervades even the most perfect wedding day. This is the most engaging human drama imaginable.

Brides today may change words, sentences, even the entire phrasing of the ceremony. Feminist Elizabeth Cady defied her father, Judge

Jewish wedding under a huppah, *or canopy.*

The Wedding Party, 1932, *by James van der Zee.*

Cady, to marry Henry Stanton in 1848. Then she confirmed her independent spirit by omitting the word "obey" from her marriage vows. Others who have made the same choice include Lilian Steichen, when she married Carl Sandburg; Georgia O'Keeffe, when she married Alfred Stieglitz; Lauren Bacall, when she married Humphrey Bogart; and Lady Diana Spencer, when she married Prince Charles. Nowadays the very concept of wifely "obedience" is obsolete and the vows reflect that.

Most frequently, of course, we hear variations on the familiar greeting, "Dearly beloved, we are gathered together here in the sight of God . . ." This might include the father of the bride welcoming the guests and stating the purpose of the gathering, or the clergyman reading a statement prepared by the bride and groom.

And then the couple, each in turn, pronounce their vows and make their promises:

from this day forward,
for better for worse,
for richer for poorer,
in sickness and in health,
to love and to cherish,
till death us do part . . .

"I do!"
"I will!"

In every language, the words of commitment echo around the world.

Celebrating Families

Happily there aren't as many in-law jokes these days. Why? Because the contemporary approach to marriage has contributed—at least in most cases—to a more loving atmosphere between families and generations. Parents and siblings gather together for a wedding that honors them as well as the bride and groom. And it's the bride who sees to this, by blending family traditions, inviting the wedding party to participate, and in general enriching everyone's life.

The Unity Candle

A candle service symbolizing family unity has become increasingly popular in this decade. The bright flame of love is kindled with the light of life of the two families. Three candles are lit in turn: the bride's parents light the right, the groom's parents light the left, and the couple themselves set the center taper aflame with the light from those two.

A bride in Houston, Texas, for example, served the reception punch from her husband's family's art deco punch bowl, using an antique silver ladle that had belonged to her mother's family since before the Civil War. Another family has a "Cousins' Club" into which the new spouse is initiated at the reception.

Many brides wear heirloom lace or carry their family Bible. Others plan their weddings around special family holy days, birthdays, or anniversaries; or they simply show their concern by choosing a wedding date that is convenient for everyone.

Brides also may honor family members by playing favorite songs at the reception, arranging special treatment for grandparents who may be infirm or disabled, and smoothing any tentative feelings of discomfort that might arise at interfaith or interracial marriages.

A father's first dance with his married daughter.

Today, because a wedding is such a family event, we welcome children of all ages as guests and participants. With their sense of fantasy, youngsters capture the spirit of the moment immediately. In fact, their enthusiastic participation has often upstaged the "star" herself. Even at Britain's recent royal wedding, the princess had to share the spotlight with her enchanting young attendants.

European brides, particularly in England and France, often have only child attendants. But the traditional role for youngsters in America is that of flower girl and ring bearer, preceding the older attendants in the processional. In deference to

Children's Roles

She stood in the corner of the bride's room, wanting to say: I love the two of you so much and you are the we of me. Please take me with you from the wedding, for we belong together . . . her tongue was heavy in her mouth and dumb. She could only speak in a voice that shook a little—to ask where was the veil?

(Carson McCullers,
The Member of the Wedding)

Betty Grable and Cesar Romero are attended by children in That Lady in Ermine.

Murphy's Law, silk petals are heaped in deep baskets, and the ring pillow has one or two "imposters" sewn on, while the honor attendants keep the real thing in their pocket.

Little girls may wear a miniature version of the bride's dress, or some charming design of silk and lace that might resemble a christening dress. Often flower girls wear an adaptation of the bridesmaids' dresses, perhaps in another color. Traditionally boys wear short pants (or kilts for Scottish clan members), but more recently fash-ion has put them in a miniature version of adult formal wear.

With second weddings there can be a complete turnaround, as older children of divorced or widowed parents actually become sponsors of the event. Today these members of a new "blended family" may greet the guests, pass out programs or packets of rice, and make toasts at the reception. And always, having a part to play can help ease the feelings of loss a child may be experiencing at the marriage of an older sibling or a parent.

"Love Is Lovelier, the Second Time Around"

Second marriages—for brides as well as bridegrooms—are a lot more commonplace now than they were years ago. Current statistics show that roughly thirty percent of all marriages are return engagements. While this is not an entirely new phenomenon (in 1947 a record number of brides married for the second time, perhaps as a result of hasty marriages during the war years), society's perception of the second-time bride has changed dramatically.

Today's repeat bride is her own woman. She has a romantic image that transcends the prejudices of the past. And she is courageous—remarrying takes strength and optimism. And yet over one million brides begin again—with a new mate —each year.

The subject of remarriage is no longer relegated to a small subsection in the appendix of etiquette books; it warrants an entire book of its own. As the community at large accepts the reality of divorce, restrictions in many faiths relax. Second-time brides are encouraged to celebrate with even more gusto. There are precious few etiquette limitations remaining. The white wedding gown, once taboo because of its virginal implications, is considered joyfully proper by all but the most conservative arbiters of taste.

Question: Should we include the children in our wedding?

Answer: Are they going to be a part of your marriage? Yes! Make them the most important part of the ceremony . . . after the vows, of course.

The remarriage of a widow is a time of optimism. Gone are the days when a widow would don a maroon "mourning dress," as she did in Colonial times. Family, friends, former in-laws, are now delighted to join in a joyous celebration that begins life anew. The bride and groom may choose whatever wedding style appeals to them, including a floor-length white dress for the bride. The veil, however, is omitted, as it is still reserved for the first-time bride.

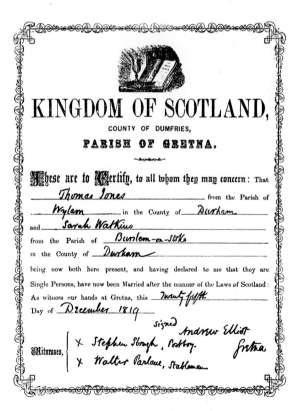

Gretna Green, in Scotland, was a famous destination for eloping couples.

Everyone in this Dutch town joins in the celebration as this wedding procession moves along the canals.

Offbeat Weddings

There are guidelines. Informal, formal, very formal, are the ways to describe the degree of elegance to which members of the wedding party—and guests—will go to fulfill their fantasies of the perfect wedding day. But the history of weddings, ranging from very traditional to nontraditional, proves how diverse these fantasies are. Couples continue to spice the celebration with personal themes and regional touches, as well as family, ethnic, or religious traditions, to make their wedding an original, creative expression of love and meaning for everyone involved.

Perhaps the bride will leave the ceremony riding sidesaddle with her bridegroom because they met on horseback. He is in full morning clothes and she is radiant in her flowing white dress, a tribute to the romanticism of the times and their image of their love.

Newspapers have carried tales of couples who married in underground caves, in prison, on motorcycles, in midair (while parachuting, with the minister administering the vows from a nearby

A bus stop where thousands begin a trip to work each day will be the scene next month of a journey of another kind—a marriage.

Jerry M. Mosier told the Transit Authority last week that he planned to marry his fiancee, Roselee, at the bus stop on Second Avenue near 82nd Street on September 9.

"It is where we met one rainy, windswept night three years ago," Mr. Mosier wrote in a letter to the authority.

At the end of the ceremony, a private bus will pull up and take the couple, together with the rest of the wedding party, to a catering hall in Brooklyn.

News of the bus stop wedding is just another reminder that despite a difficult summer, life goes on at the Transit Authority. "We do a lot more than derailments," said Karen Borack, the authority's director of public affairs.

The New York Times, 8 August 1983

airplane). Some sentimental brides have chosen to marry in the place where they met their future husband—be it at the finish line of a marathon, an airport terminal, or a high cliff overlooking the Pacific.

Others have been wed at their corporate offices (on the rolling lawns, no doubt) or under a circus tent, because that's where they worked. And there's even a wedding on record where a computer (programmed, of course, by the local clergyman) presided over the happy couple.

Brides are married in secrecy, privacy, or with great fanfare and public acknowledgment. The first wedding on radio took place in 1922 at Grand Central Palace in New York City, when two couples were united in a ceremony broadcast by station WEAF to four thousand listeners. Television too has had its share of weddings, including the high-Neilsen nuptials of Tiny Tim and Miss Vicki, who were wed on the *Tonight Show* in the late 1960s.

Ceremonies may even unite participants who aren't necessarily standing side by side . . . first in 1900 by telegraph between Kansas City, Missouri, and a town in Oklahoma; in 1920 by a ship-to-shore radio between a sailor on the U.S.S. *Birmingham* in the Pacific and his bride in Michigan; and in 1933 by transatlantic telephone, when a bride in Sweden married the love of her life while he was still in Detroit.

A Memento for the Future

Whatever the time, place, style of the wedding, the bride and groom will cherish a photographic record of their day, whether it's a scrapbook of snapshots taken by enthusiastic friends or a leather-bound volume produced by a professional wedding photographer.

The earliest known photograph of a bride in her wedding dress is a daguerreotype taken in Boston in 1854. A century ago wedding pictures were often finished in small prints, similar to visiting cards. But there were few practitioners skilled in the art of photography, and as late as 1938 in a large city like Los Angeles, there was only one man who specialized in taking wedding pictures.

The style of early photographs was dramatic and "painterly." At first bridal portraits were taken at home. Later, sittings were arranged in the studio where lights and equipment assured professional results. Candid photography became widespread only after World War II, and then the wedding became a story to record.

As the wedding album became more and more popular in the United States, the practice of recording minute details increased. At first photographers were forbidden to snap pictures inside the church and had to content themselves with candids before and after the ceremony, missing the high point of the event. Now, the passion for recording every moment, every emotion, on film can be satisfied (if the church allows it). The entire day—ceremony, reception, the works—may be videotaped. As more people possess video recorders, the percentage of taped weddings (only one out of fifteen now) will probably increase. Indeed, the bride and her bridegroom are stars at their own show . . . with the footage, if not the ratings, to prove it!

OPPOSITE *The traditional arch of swords can take many forms, depending upon the groom's profession.*

6
The Reception

The Guests are met, the feast is set, may'st hear the merry din.

(Samuel Coleridge, "Rime of the Ancient Mariner")

The time and style of the wedding ceremony usually determine the type of reception. A morning wedding is often followed by a breakfast or brunch. A light buffet of sandwiches and cake might be served after an afternoon wedding—or a picnic might be in order after an informal outdoor wedding. Guests at late afternoon and evening weddings are usually invited to a seated dinner—which can be anything from a simple casserole to a multicourse banquet.

Whatever form it takes, the wedding reception is a happy celebration to honor, bless, and rejoice in the commitment of love made by the bride and groom.

The festivities begin with the receiving line, which bridges ceremony and reception and sets the celebration in motion. The custom allows the newlyweds to greet all their guests with a handshake or kiss, and gives the guests an opportunity to wish the couple well. It may also hark back to the belief that on her wedding day the bride is blessed, and that touching or kissing her brings good luck.

At a large wedding, the receiving line can be long and time-consuming. It's a considerate host who fortifies his guests with champagne, some hors d'oeuvres, and perhaps a little music while they wait! On the other hand, at a casual reception such as a barbecue or at a small breakfast, the bride and groom may greet the guests informally, then "make the rounds," spending a few minutes with each guest before sitting down themselves.

Food, Drink, and Keeping the Devil at Bay

Years ago, wedding celebrations often lasted for days or even weeks. Indulging in food and drink created an atmosphere of plenty, a promise of fortune and fertility shared by guests and the bride and groom. The largesse exhibited at medieval weddings was extraordinary; beggars would gleefully follow the wedding procession from church to hall, knowing that the hosts would share with them the leftovers from the feast.

The importance attached to food and drink in wedding celebrations has its origins in antiquity.

The largest dish ever prepared was a roasted camel—for a Bedouin wedding. The camel was prepared in the following way:

> eggs were stuffed into fish,
>
> fish were stuffed into chickens,
>
> chickens were stuffed into a roasted lamb,
>
> the lamb was stuffed inside the whole camel.

The entire camel was roasted and served to the assembled wedding guests.

Guinness Book of World Records

A peasant bride and groom symbolically begin to share a life with their first meal.

At one time, in fact, the sharing of a particular food or wine often constituted the entire marriage ritual. The Britons, for example, drank marriage-mead for thirty days as their nuptial rite. (The word *bridal* is derived from "bride-ale.")

The ancient Greeks believed that the newly married pair had to eat a quince together to promote their love. In accepting a fruit that was both bitter and sweet, the bride was symbolically agreeing to accept her husband "for better for worse."

In Bali, couples first made offerings of food and flowers to the gods, then consummated their marriage before the offerings faded, and only after that was the wedding ceremony held.

The sharing of special wedding foods continues today. In a Japanese wedding, the bride and groom drink sake as an important part of the ritual. In Brittany, the couple drink brandy and eat white bread. A Turkish bride and groom nibble sweetmeats from each other's lips, and German newlyweds share a bowl of soup.

Champagne to Celebrate

No matter what other beverages are served at the reception—and no matter how informal the party may be—it's traditional today to toast the bride and groom with champagne. It is champagne, the sparkling wine that is synonymous with romance and gaiety, that has come to symbolize bridal joy —so much so, in fact, that today the wedding toast is often referred to as a champagne toast.

Named for the region in France where the wine is produced, champagne was first made by a blind monk, Dom Pérignon, who was the cellar master of a Benedictine abbey and whose name today identifies a coveted brand of champagne. Pérignon found that wine would begin to sparkle if left to ferment for several years in a tightly sealed container. "I am drinking the stars," he shouted after sampling his new effervescent creation.

The discovery attracted considerable popularity, and all the kings and emperors, and with them the aristocracy of Europe, became enamored of champagne. Madame de Pompadour said that champagne was the only drink that leaves a woman still beautiful after drinking it. Marie Antoinette was so enchanted with the pleasure of champagne that she had a glass specially designed following the contour of her breast!

Today champagne is more commonly served in

A Memorable Wedding Toast

The first recorded toast was given at a Saxon feast in 450 A.D. by a woman who by the evening's end became a bride. British King Vortigern was so moved by the sentiment (a simple "Lord King, be of health!") offered by Rowena, daughter of the Saxon leader Hengist, that he proceeded to make passionate love to her. Intoxicated by drink, possibly love, and definitely greed, he then bargained with Hengist for her hand. A deal was arranged whereby Hengist received the province of Kent in exchange for Rowena. Vortigern and Rowena were married that same evening. Apparently no further toasts were offered!

the wine. The celebratory aura champagne brings to a reception and all other pre- and postwedding festivities can instantly create a feeling of *la bonne vie*—the good life.

To Health, to Life, to Love! As champagne-filled glasses are raised, a tangible sense of excitement fills the room. Speeches are made, best wishes expressed to the bride and groom, and then glass touches glass, and a chorus of clinks heralds a festive time for all.

Two newlywed couples toast each other.
Below: Shirley Temple and Sgt. John Agar.

Toasts from the Groom to the Bride

Here's to the prettiest, here's to the wittiest,
Here's to the truest of all who are true,
Here's to the neatest one, here's to the sweetest one,
Here's to them all in one—here's to you.

Here's to the woman that I love
And here's to the woman that loves me,
And here's to all those that love her that I love,
And to those that love her that love me.

flute- or tulip-shaped glasses to keep the bubbles rising, at a cool temperature to ensure sparkle and fragrance, and after a gentle uncorking to save the froth and increase the pleasure of drinking

The long round of toasts begins in Silver Dollar, *featuring Edward G. Robinson and Bebe Daniels.*

By affirming the toast through the touching of glasses, guests send an unspoken yet audible message to the bride and groom—a message that the ancients directed to none other than the devil! The intention was to produce a bell-like sound so as to banish the devil, who is repelled by bells.

There is another explanation for glasses clinking. Wine lovers have long believed that in order to get the greatest pleasure from a drink, all five senses should come into play. Wine is meant to be tasted, touched, seen, smelled—and heard.

Many people end wedding toasts the way the ancients did, by breaking wineglasses or other objects, which takes us back to the devil: it was another way to scare off evil spirits.

Although people had been drinking to one another for centuries, toasting as a formal practice did not appear until the sixteenth century. At feasts given by French noblemen, it was customary to drink to the health of one of the ladies. Then a piece of toast was placed in the bottom of a goblet of wine, which was passed around. The last to receive it—the honored lady—got to eat the wine-soaked toast and receive everyone's compliments. Thus a courtly custom became known as a "toast."

While it's traditionally the best man who makes the first toast, any of the wedding guests may follow with their personal heartfelt expressions. Parents, grandparents, and—in the case of remarriage—children may relish the chance to share their warm, happy wishes.

A seventeen-year-old Pennsylvania boy raised his glass and proposed this toast to his new stepfather: "I'd like to propose a toast to Michael, who's Mom's new husband today. When you first showed up, Jennie and I didn't like you very much. I mean, you were different, you know. And you wore a vest. But now that we've gotten to know you, we've seen you hit a baseball as good as the next guy. And, well, what I want to say is, welcome to our house . . . Dad."

May their joys be as deep as the ocean
And their misfortunes as light as the foam.

• • •

Let us toast the health of the bride;
Let us toast the health of the groom,
Let us toast the person that tied;
Let us toast every guest in the room.

• • •

A toast to love and laughter,
and happily ever after.

The bride and groom in turn may want to honor parents, grandparents, and attendants in special tributes. And toasting has always acknowledged the importance of marriage to the community. Thus, when a couple honor their guests with this standard refrain, "To all the people we know and all the people we'll never know whose lives made our lives together possible," they are perpetuating a custom as old as it is seemingly modern.

Some take their gold
In minted mold,
And some in harps hereafter,
But give me mine
In bubbles fine
And keep the change in laughter.

Oliver Herford

Wedding Cakes, Plain and Fancy

In every wedding album, there is a picture of the bride and groom cutting their wedding cake. And it's no wonder that this special moment is remembered, cherished, documented for posterity —for it is the sweet summit of the wedding reception, for guests as well as the couple.

The wedding cake can be traced back to ancient Rome, where a simple wheat cake or biscuit was broken during the wedding ceremony and the first morsels eaten by the bride and groom. The remainder of the cake was crumbled over the bride's head as a fertility rite—to guarantee the couple many children and a life of plenty.

At Elizabethan weddings, guests would stack small sweet buns to form a centerpiece. They would then issue a playful challenge to the bride and groom to kiss over the stacked mound, to guarantee good luck. Then in the seventeenth century a French chef was inspired to frost the small cakes with white sugar so they would hold together and stand upright, and thus was created the forebear of the tiered wedding cake we know today.

The traditional white wedding cake, or "bride's cake," first appeared in the United States about the time of the Civil War. Until then, the American wedding cake resembled the standard British one: a dark, spicy fruitcake. By the mid-1800s, however, the introduction of finely ground flour and the manufacture of baking powder and baking soda led to the creation of the white wedding cake. The fruitcake became known as the "groom's cake" and continued to be served along with the bride's cake.

Today wedding cakes seem to be limited only by the bride and groom's imagination. Shapes and flavors reflect their personalities. Cakes can resemble a wedding ring or a church, a bell or a heart; they can be round, square, tiered, or flat. Flavors can vary from basic poundcake to pecan, strawberry, mocha, coconut, orange, or chocolate. Health-conscious couples may choose carrot cake or health breads (pumpkin, lemon, banana). Couples marrying a second time may decide on a country look—a romantic three-tiered delight with soft pastel flowers, fondant or real, cascading from the top.

A Japanese couple surveys the tiers of a fragile cake.

Heritage often determines the selection. A bride and groom of French background may have a caramel-frosted tower of cream puffs, called *croquembouche,* a carryover from the seventeenth-century mounds of small cakes. In a Greek wedding, the bride and groom traditionally eat a cake baked with sesame seeds, honey, and quince to symbolize that they are marrying for better or worse. Italians fete a newly married couple with a rum-filled cream cake; Americans can honor

their frontier roots with a "stack cake," a layered cake sandwiched with applesauce.

The elaborate decoration of wedding cakes dates to Victorian times, when confectioners vied with one another in creating ostentatious displays for society and royal weddings. One stunning ex-

---

Cakes to Top It Off

- Queen Victoria's wedding cake weighed 300 pounds, measured 3 yards across and 14 inches high, and was decorated with roses. Atop the cake was an ice sculpture of Britannia, surrounded by cupids.

- Actress Rita Hayworth eschewed the traditional silver cake knife for a dramatic glass sword. The reception, in June 1949, took place at the Riviera home of groom Aly Khan.

- When Grace Kelly married Prince Rainier of Monaco in 1956, a replica of a crown sat elegantly atop the cake. At her daughter Caroline's wedding in 1978, a pair of caged doves served as the cake topper. Caroline defied a wedding superstition by serving the first piece of her chocolate wedding cake to the Mayor of Monaco, instead of to her groom, French businessman Phillipe Junot. The couple's marriage ended shortly after in divorce.

- At the 1966 White House wedding of Luci Baines Johnson to Patrick Nugent, the icing on their fourteen-tier, 300-pound "summer fruit cake" yielded only after several attempts by bride, groom, and the President himself.

- When actor Jack Webb, star of the television police series *Dragnet,* got married, his cake was decorated entirely with police badges made out of sugar icing. The cake was so immense that it had to be sawed in half to fit through the doors to the reception hall.

ample was the wedding cake for Queen Victoria's
fourth daughter, Princess Louise. Its lower tier
contained baskets of flowers and fruit; the second
was festooned with roses (for England), sham-
rocks (for Ireland), and thistles (for Scotland); the
third was wrapped in network with cornucopias
and monogrammed shields. The entire cake was

The couple (right) begins the ritual of cake-cutting
with a kiss, while the groom (below)
feeds his new wife the first bite.

I sing of brooks, of blossoms, birds, and bowers:
Of April, May, of June, and July-flowers.
I sing of May-poles, Hock-carts, wassails, wakes,
Of bride-grooms, brides, and of their bridal cakes.

Robert Herrick,
"The Argument of His Book"

crowned with a vase of flowers and silk banners edged in silver fringe.

Today's exquisite wedding cakes blend traditional adornments with personal designs: wedding bells, cupids, and lovebirds of spun sugar; delicate orange blossoms, white roses; tiny flags and horseshoes are some traditional selections. Nontraditional decorations might be balloons floating skyward from the tiers of cake, or a trellis or tic-tac-toe game etched on the white icing. And many couples forego bridal-white icing in favor of a cake of many hues, to create a rainbow or patchwork-quilt effect.

Cake Superstitions

• A bride should never bake her own wedding cake; this brings bad luck.

• A bride who steals a taste of wedding cake before it is cut forfeits her husband's love. However, saving a fragment ensures his lifelong fidelity.

• A bridesmaid who carries wedding cake in her pocket until the bride and groom's honeymoon is over will soon marry.

• After the first wedding in a family, part of the wedding cake must be kept in the house until all the unmarried daughters are wed, to ensure a husband for each.

Small figures of a bride and groom are standard ornaments on top of the cake; other choices include miniature wooden boats, tiny tennis rackets, blown-glass animals—objects that represent shared interests of the bride and groom. For an edible topping, many brides choose chocolate petals or ripe strawberries. Fresh flowers, perhaps arranged to resemble the bride's bouquet, can crown a cake—naturally. In Bermuda, where baking the cake becomes a community project, a tree seedling tops the cake and later is planted by the couple.

The groom's cake, traditionally fruitcake, can also be chocolate, spice, mocha, or carrot. Sometimes it is iced in white and used as the top layer of the bride's cake. More commonly, though, the groom's cake is sliced in advance and packed in individual boxes for guests to take home and possibly use as "dreaming bread." An old superstition suggests that single guests who place a sliver of groom's cake under their pillows will dream of their future spouse.

A bride and groom, relaxed after the ceremony, enjoy their reception, hamming it up for the camera.

Wedding Favors

Elizabethan brides had a happy custom of giving bows and love knots of lace or ribbon as favors to guests. One eighteenth-century mother wanted ribbons (ribands), to make an impression at her son's wedding.

> Do ask . . . whether we may go colours flying tomorrow—that is to say, whether any objection lies to our bedecking our folks with favours, namely, cockades of white riband in their hats, for we think it would look mighty pretty along the High Road and announce to the people that we are a joyful train, and make them stare and say "Who's that?"

The Early Married Life of Maria Josepha Lady Stanley, 1796, edited by Hane H. Adeane

Nowadays, couples still enjoy giving favors as a way of sharing their special day with their guests. Italians proffer almonds in tulle packages, as symbols of the bitter and sweet aspects of life. Japanese and Russian brides and grooms may give tiny picture frames, bud vases, sachets, even more costly gifts—to express their appreciation for their friends' and families' support. American couples frequently offer each departing guest a tiny monogrammed box containing a piece of wedding cake and tied with a white satin ribbon.

Other favors offered by American brides to their guests:

- Seasonal favorites—decorated Easter eggs or sparkling Christmas ornaments to add holiday spirit.
- After a late wedding, a "box breakfast" of a favorite regional or ethnic food, along with the Sunday paper.
- An instant wedding photo of the bride and groom with a frame to put it in.
- Wedding memorabilia: wedding programs, complete with vows, music, readings, names of wedding party members; matchbooks and menus embossed with the couple's names and the wedding date; breakaway bouquets or small potted plants from table centerpieces.

Music and Dancing

Music is the thread that weaves all the parts of the reception together. It can move a receiving line along at a good pace, create an anticipatory mood for the cake-cutting ceremony, and inspire an epidemic of "happy feet" among guests on the dance floor.

From the medieval minstrels who serenaded the bride and groom with lute and cymbals to the turn-of-the-century itinerant musician who led a country wedding procession to the sweet strains of his fiddle, music has accompanied the bride and groom through the ages.

Today string quartets, jazz combos, small orchestras, bluegrass bands, or the latest records and

This Mexican clay sculpture celebrates the community spirit of a village wedding.

Enter the Waltz

One form of German folk dance was known as the "wooing dance." It involved a tight embrace to steady the partner during the dance's rapid turns, as well as stolen kisses in what was an unabashed wooing of the dance partner. Out of this dance of lovers came the waltz.

The waltz was a departure from the stylized "court dances" that were fashionable with the European aristocracy through the eighteenth century. The minuet, quadrille, and contredanse involved a rigid sequence of steps and, at the very most, a light clasping of hands.

The expressive, spirited waltz swept the nineteenth-century world off its feet, gaining acceptance among all levels of society. The breathless turns of the dance, allowing couples to lose themselves in each other's arms, continue their intoxicating hold on today's brides and grooms.

tapes entertain guests. Music sets a mood, an atmosphere, a tone for the wedding party. For an intimate celebration, a piano, a trio of violins, or an accordion might provide the perfect background music. For a large, lavish wedding, a band or orchestra that can perform everything from old standards and country ballads to pop, rock, and disco may be best. In 1947, one couple hired a dance band, a chamber music ensemble, a strolling gypsy guitarist, a violinist, an accordionist,

At a Greek wedding reception, the couple and their guests have a chance to rekindle the traditions of old folk dances and songs. The warmth and vitality of family life continues.

and the Firestone radio singers to cater to their wedding guests' every musical whim!

Ancient wedding dances were communal and symbolic. In a German bridal round known as "dancing the bride out," the bride would stand in the center of a double circle—young women on the inside, young men on the outside—while the groom had to force his way through both circles to gain his bride. In the "dance of the old wives," all the married women danced with the bride to officially welcome her into their community. Another old custom had the bride circle the fireplace or pothook three times, to symbolize her taking possession of her new home.

Even as the forms of dance evolved through the ages and mixed, or couple, dancing was introduced, the early story-telling dances lived on in spirit through folk dancing. Today at Greek weddings in Cyprus, guests regale the bride and

groom with dances that tell old fairy tales. The tarantella, the polka, the jig, the czarda, and the horah are all familiar ethnic dances which add vitality and meaning to a present-day celebration.

Many ritual wedding dances are associated with fire—a life-giving force. For instance, Mexican wedding couples danced around a fire with their clothes tied together, to represent marital and community unity. In Java (Indonesia), the grandparents, holding fire fans, passed on their power to the newlyweds in a special dance.

The circle pattern, which symbolizes the roundness of life and the wholeness of the community, is common in ethnic dances. In the Jewish *mitzvah tantz*, the bride is seated in the center of a circle of guests who dance around her, then lift her, chair and all. And to honor parents when their last unmarried daughter weds, Jews tradionally link hands for the *mizinka*. In the Greek

Kilts and skirts fly in a Scottish wedding dance.

A Washington, D.C. bride turned her three-block trip from cathedral to reception into a community event. Bagpipes led the wedding assemblage, as neighbors came out to watch and others joined in the fun.

In Summit, New Jersey, a bride lined the few streets between church and country club with potted chrysanthemums to resemble a royal parade route.

handkerchief dance, the leader and his partner hold corners of a handkerchief, and all link hands and dance in a circle.

The bride and groom's first dance—one of the most romantic and symbolic moments in contemporary weddings, representing the start of a new life together—has its roots in history.

In ancient Prussia when the King attended a wedding, his royal torches were used to lead the procession and light the wedding room. The bride and groom began the dance. Then the bride danced with the King, and next with the princes and all other male guests, beginning with the oldest. The groom also danced with all the women, according to the same protocol. The idea was that the bride and groom should each gather strength from the community before retiring to the bedchamber. (At a very large wedding this might have been counterproductive!)

Today the waltz is the traditional first dance of the bride and groom and although the King is not usually present, a certain order follows. After their first dance together, the bride dances with her father and the groom with his mother, and after the family members have all had a turn the guests join in. Following the first few waltzes, other current dances may take over—foxtrot, jitterbug, rhumba, whatever is popular.

Prankish friends of the groom celebrate his change of marital status by playing a practical joke—a shower of paper greets his declaration and mocks the scandalized faces of the wedding party.

Fun and Games

At the heart of every wedding celebration is a sense of revelry and exuberant spirit, and one of the ways it is expressed is through games and amusements. Pageants and masques were the order of the day at Elizabethan weddings; modern weddings substitute joke-telling, group singing, even staged skits. The court poet would recite an epithalamium, a song or poem in honor of the bride and groom; the best man reading out the telegrams of congratulations is his twentieth-century counterpart. The Elizabethans engaged in hunts and tournaments as wedding sport; these have been replaced with tamer outdoor pursuits

such as croquet, badminton, and even frisbee-throwing.

Races were a popular wedding sport in the eighteenth and nineteenth centuries, and they are still customary in Ireland, Scotland, and Germany. A reminder of the days of bride-capture, "young man races," as they were called, involved the men of the bridal party and friends. Races would usually start at the church and end at the reception hall, thus getting the wedding festivities off to a spirited start.

Throwing the garter is a custom derived from an old British ritual called "flinging the stocking": guests invaded the bridal chamber, and the women grabbed the groom's stockings while the

The toss of the bouquet remains one of the most romantic wedding games. It promises another would-be bride her day to star.

men stole the bride's. They took turns flinging the stockings; and whoever threw the one which landed on the bride's or groom's nose would be the next to marry! By the fourteenth century, the bride's garter had become so highly esteemed that the bride would frequently be rushed at the altar by throngs of guests competing for the prize. In self-preservation, she began to remove the garter herself to throw to the crowds. Hence today's custom of the groom throwing the bride's garter to the unmarried men at the reception.

The toss of the bride's bouquet is one of the most eagerly awaited reception games. Tradition has it that the woman who catches the bouquet will be the next to marry. In the United States in the 1800s, the bride would throw a series of small bouquets, one to each of her bridesmaids. In one

a ring was hidden, and the woman who caught that bouquet would be next to wed. As part of the bouquet-tossing ritual, the bride, to be impartial, must turn her back to the crowd of hopefuls. Still, it comes as no surprise when a sister or close friend catches it. When Luci Johnson threw her bouquet at her White House wedding in 1966, her sister, Lynda, was the lucky recipient.

Departure games and customs signal the winding down of the reception. Actually, guests in olden times never saw the bride and groom off as is done today. Rather, they escorted them to their wedding-night quarters, where they helped to undress the bride and groom and properly tuck them into their marriage bed. This was a not-so-subtle way of reminding the couple of their responsibility to the community to create a family.

Sparkling Wedding Customs

- After Jewish newlyweds drink from a wine glass, the groom crushes it underfoot, a reminder of the destruction of the temple in Jerusalem and a portent of his future prowess.

- Lithuanians are served a symbolic meal by their parents—wine for joy, salt for tears, and bread for work.

- Early Americans gave the newlyweds energy with sack posset—hot spiced milk and brew—at the wedding party.

- Greek Orthodox couples sip wine three times, symbolizing the Trinity.

- Young Irishmen raced from the church to the bride's house to win a bottle of ale. The groom poured out the last drops for good fortune.

- In China, goblets of wine and honey are tied together with red string (for joy), and the couple exchange a drink.

Guests prepare the bride and groom for their wedding night.

A grand exit for this English fireman and his bride aboard a fire engine, for once on a joyful errand.

When they're ready to make their grand escape from the reception, many couples find that their car has been gaily decorated by friends and family with crepe paper and streamers, with tin cans and old shoes dangling from the bumper. The old shoes are a reminder of an early Anglo-American marriage ritual. As part of the wedding dowry, a shoe or slipper of the bride was given to the groom, who would nail it to the wall over the marriage bed. This signified the transference of authority over the bride to the new husband.

Tin cans, horns, and other noisemakers were meant to protect the bride and groom while traveling. The racket they created would keep evil spirits away from the newlyweds, who were thought to be particularly vulnerable in transit. These traditions live on today, as exhibited in the sight and sound of honeymoon vehicles, assuring the bride and groom Godspeed as they head off for their new life together.

Royal Send-off

After a fairy-tale wedding that cast a spell around the world, Princess Diana and Prince Charles left for their honeymoon in more ordinary style. The Prince's brothers, Andrew and Edward, scrawled "Just Married" on a piece of cardboard with lipstick purloined from a lady-in-waiting and attached the notice to the back of the carriage—along with some blue and silver heart-shaped balloons saved from a pre-wedding gala—to announce the news to all the royal subjects.

A Ford converted into a princely wedding chariot, complete with prancing horses,
bears the young Indian couple away in Hyderabad.

Newlyweds on the Grand Canal, Venice.

A flower-bedecked buggy waits for the bridal pair in a scene of simple charm.

7
The Honeymoon—and After

"Tell me about your honeymoon," everyone says to the new bride. It is not surprising that people are so interested, for the honeymoon has always been the most romantic way station in the bride's passage from woman to wife.

To the ancients, the moon had connotations of impermanence. Weddings would be unlucky, they believed, if they occurred during the waning of the moon. The "moon" of the honeymoon reminded couples that within a month—as the phases of the moon changed—things could alter and diminish. In any case the moon was fickle and inconstant. The "honey" refers to a drink of fermented honey called mead, or metheglin. Early Germanic tribesmen, who used to capture their brides from neighboring villages, enjoyed the intoxicating effects of this brew. Consumed by bride and groom for the thirty days of the moon's cycle, it had the effect of keeping the world at bay for the young couple during the month of changes.

Today, though the reasons might be different, not much has changed; couples still keep to themselves during this "getting used to each other" phase. In this period of adjustment, a man and woman make the psychological shift from being single to being married. It is a unique time in a couple's life, when they are allowed to be totally private, secluded, and carefree. Philip Slater, social critic, suggests that the wedding and the honeymoon each foster an essential bond. The former fosters the tie to society, enabling the couple to understand their role in the collective life of the community; the latter fosters the intimacy between the man and the woman that will bond them in a cohesive relationship.

The community has its own not-so-subtle ways of indicating to the couple that they should not become too self-absorbed. Honeymoon pranks are an example. Consider some of the familiar gags: decorating the get-away car, hiding or removing the luggage from it, flattening the

> The little house was not far away, and the only bridal journey Meg had was the quiet walk with John, from the old home to the new. When she came down, looking like a pretty Quakeress in her dove-colored suit and straw bonnet tied with white, they all gathered about her to say "good-by," as tenderly as if she had been going to make the grand tour. . . .
>
> They stood watching her, with faces full of love and hope and tender pride, as she walked away, leaning on her husband's arm, with her hands full of flowers, and the June sunshine brightening her happy face,—and so Meg's married life began.
>
> Louisa Mae Alcott, *Little Women*

tires, tying noisy cans to the bumper. All of this mischief is designed to make it more difficult for the couple to go off on their own. Once they reach their destination, the disturbances to the honeymooners' privacy continue. Phone calls throughout the night, room service deliveries that appear unexpectedly, the charivari (or shivaree)— a raucous serenade under the window—all send the message: "You're still a part of us."

In the Middle Ages, consummation of the

marriage was likely to take place before the couple ever left the wedding celebration. Afterward, instead of a honeymoon trip, a procession to the couple's new home would take place.

In earlier times, the bride's passage to her new life was dramatic. The Athenian bride was driven to her groom's house in a chariot. The axle was then burned or broken—to sever her ties to her old life with her family and to keep her, literally without wheels, at the home of her groom.

But the bride of old was more tethered than severed, since the village or tribe was really an extended family. Moving to a new home within the clan was not moving too far away geographically. Today's bride may experience more of an actual wrenching away from her family, since mobility and job relocation often take her far from her hometown.

The Spirits That Lurk

In the ancient world, evil spirits were very real. Since there were few scientific explanations when things suddenly went wrong, it was believed that the spirits brought death, disease, and bad crops. It is no wonder, then, that the innocent and pure bride seemed a particularly vulnerable target, one who had to be protected.

When the couple reached their new home, the groom carried his bride over the threshold in order to avoid those demons that might be lurking on the doorstep, and to keep the bride from tracking any evil spirits in on the soles of her feet.

In Hungary, an old custom is still observed in some villages. Wedding guests escort the bride and groom to their bridal bedroom, then dance around the house nine times to drive away any

Carrying the bride over the threshold.

evil spirits that may be waiting there. The next day, a married woman's cap is placed on the bride's head. A small fire is then lit in the village square and everyone dances around it. The bride, however, jumps over the flames, thus evading the demons, as final insurance that she will not be bewitched.

There are other examples of brides and grooms in various cultures taking precautions against the intrusion of evil spirits into their lives at this most crucial time. During the marriage consummation, a Moroccan bridegroom may place a dagger between the sheets of the bridal bed to keep evil spirits away.

Medieval Christians were superstitious too. A priest came to bless the bridal bed and sprinkle holy water on the bride and groom. He then censed the room to drive off the demons it was believed would be attracted by the sexual act. Today, many Christian clergymen will visit the couple's new home for a house blessing, a lovely custom that sanctifies it, or sets it apart, as a place where a very special union can take place.

The Marriage Bed

Getting ready for bed can be awkward when couples have not already been sexually intimate. But there was no stalling in the bathroom for the medieval bride and her groom! Their friends waltzed them right into the bedchamber and helped them into their dressing gowns. Loosening the knots of the bride's garments symbolically made the loss of her virginity easier.

The nuptial bed was prepared by family and friends of the bride and groom in ways that ensured good luck. After all, there were imminent dangers—the ever-lurking evil spirits, the possibility that the breaking of the bride's hymen might be painful, or worse yet, the discovery that the bride might not prove to be a virgin. So the wedding party surrounded the bed with symbols of successful defloration, such as the color red, which symbolized the drops of red blood. The Chinese hung three strips of red paper from the bed's canopy. The Greeks and Romans dressed the bed in red satin sheets. The Finns covered the newlyweds with a red blanket, but left nice white sheets on the mattress, so the couple (and probably the family) could see the results of their lovemaking.

Other strange things turned up in the marriage bed, often as fertility symbols. For example, the parents of an Oriental Jewish bride traditionally tucked a raw fish between the sheets. A Peruvian

A honeymoon toast in their own heart-shaped tub is a romantic prelude to a new life.

bridal party decorated the honeymoon bed with red and green chili peppers. And the father of a French peasant bride put a long loaf of bread into bed with the couple. Besides being an obvious symbol of plenty, the crumpled state of the bread in the morning gave *le père* some indication of what had gone on the night before!

Sexual intercourse was once an imperative of the honeymoon; proof of the marriage consummation was extremely important in primitive cultures. Today it continues to be important in countries where bride-price is based on virginity.

Historically, the activity in the nuptial bedchamber proceeded in a prescribed way. Moslems and some Christians used to abstain from sex for a period of time after the wedding; "Tobias Nights," for instance, lasted three days and were designed to prevent the devil from entering the new bride. In other cultures, sexual intercourse took place on the wedding night, even being witnessed by the best man in some Slavic and Russian bedrooms. The best man in some ancient cultures deflowered the bride himself. His motives were altruistic: he acted to spare the bridegroom, for intercourse was a mysterious act, linked to the gods of procreation, and the blood that resulted from the breaking of the bride's hymen was greatly feared.

In many cultures, members of the wedding party found ways to be helpful. The Serbs hurled glasses, pots, anything handy, against a target—a burlap sack containing an egg—hung from the bedchamber door. When the egg was finally broken (along with the glassware and china!), it was assumed that the marriage had been consummated. Amongst the Teutons of early Germany, and in parts of Sicily today, the bedclothes, bearing evidence of the consummation of the marriage and the defloration of the bride, were displayed. In Cyprus relatives still stand outside the bridal house on the morning following the wedding night, waiting for the bridegroom to come to the window and announce that all is well —or that all is not well. If things are not as they should be, the bride's mother wears her kerchief low on her forehead and goes about in silence all day. If everything is fine, she wears her kerchief high on her head to indicate pride.

Aphrodisiacs

Aphrodite, the Greek goddess of love, devised the first aphrodisiac—a food, drink, or drug to enhance desire. There must have been something to these concoctions, for the Ecclesiastical Council of Treves in 1310 branded them heretical!

Still, all over the world people have their trusted *aide-amours*. When in Rome, order up almonds, but in other places and other times, other remedies:

- Orient—ginseng, a root shaped like a small man
- Ancient Greece—carrots
- Switzerland—cheese
- Africa—yohimbine, from the bark of a tree
- France—truffles or tomatoes
- England—seafood, especially oysters
- Europe (Middle Ages)—sesame seeds soaked in beaten sparrow's eggs, cooked in milk
- Arabia—twenty almonds and one hundred grains of pine nuts mixed in a glass of honey

If the groom was displeased with his bride, she might be sent back like unsatisfactory merchandise and the bride-price would be returned. But if he was pleased, he might give her a "morning gift" as a sign of his pleasure, perhaps a necklace or a lovely dress. The custom is an old one, and in Europe the gifts increased in value over the years until at last men of noble birth were giving large estates after a successful wedding night. Emperor Otto of Germany gave his new bride, Princess Eadgyth, the city of Magdeburg as a morning gift!

There is a charming Danish custom whereby the groom puts a small present under the bride's pillow the morning after the wedding. This is not an evaluation of her performance, but a token of his love with which to begin the first day of married life. In the 1930s in the United States there was a popular custom called "Fleur du Jour." Each day of the new marriage—or week, or anniversary—was marked by the arrival via Western Union of a tiny flower box containing a red or white carnation or a blue cornflower, a boutonnière for the groom's lapel.

The Bridal Tour

In the nineteenth century, going away for a few days of seclusion expanded into the "bridal tour" (for the affluent), and soon the honeymoon became popular with most couples.

Many wealthy newlyweds elaborated even further on the honeymoon, turning it into a glamorous wedding tour, as lavish as a six-month cruise or travels throughout Europe. At the very least, well-to-do couples spent several days at a fine hotel in the nearest big city.

The Trousseau

Along with the glamorous tours went the purchase of expensive new clothes for the bride, who had to dress for her role as a married woman. Even today, collecting her trousseau can be the shopping spree of the bride's lifetime. In many places—the United States, France, Canada—the bride is feted at a "trousseau tea" prior to her wedding where she shows off her lovely lingerie to her women friends. The trousseau (from the French word *trousse,* which means "bundle") originally included all the possessions that the bride took with her to the marriage. In Greece, a donkey wreathed in flowers, with the bride's belongings tied to its back, made the trip to the newlyweds' house. In rural Italy, an open cart displayed the housewares.

Trousseaus had become so extravagant by the mid-1800s that many a groom was nearly frightened away at the prospect of keeping his wife in such a lavish manner. One male lament was published in *The Tatler* in 1877:

> Propound to her the question of marriage and you will speedily arrive at the truth of the fact. You will find she has not a single article of attire from a night cap to a shoe lace; but must first be replaced and then reduplicated; and the trousseau with all its horrors, rises before you as the first female bar to matrimony. True, you will (probably) not have to pay for it yourself but it will be the first shadow of a fearful burden you must bear all the rest of your life and its monstrous proportions indicate a Giant Horror from which you will shrink back appalled. Why a girl cannot be married "all standing" has ever been a mystery to us but as a matter of fact she WILL not go to church without an entirely new rigout and as she is on her wedding day so you will be expected to keep her hence forth and for ever.

At one time, the trousseau would have been mostly handmade. Young girls began sewing at an

A gown from a nineteenth-century wedding trousseau.

A $10.00 BRIDAL SUIT FOR $4.75

Modeled from the French. It includes Gown, Skirt, Chemise, Drawers and Corset Cover. It is exquisite in pattern, perfect in detail, and withal a price wonder. If it only serves to introduce you to the
liveliest store for Dry Goods in Chicago and the best Underwear Department west of New York, it will
have answered a good purpose. We have a unique Catalogue for Spring—yours for the asking. Address

SCHLESINGER & MAYER, Chicago

early age, learning stitches for cutwork and em-
broidery on bed linens, learning how to quilt—
and finally, making their trousseau clothing.
Their mothers and other female relatives would
help.

Some wealthy Americans traveled to Europe
by steamship to go to the couturiers—such as the
House of Worth in Paris—for custom fittings for
wedding and trousseau attire. Expensive as the
process was, these exquisitely made clothes would
last a lifetime.

Things only got worse. By 1930 *The Bride's
Book—Young Housewife's Compendium* advised
that a bride needed a dozen of everything! But
unless the bride was very rich, or very busy, she
might temper this extravagance by making her
own lingerie.

From her trousseau, the bride selected her
honeymoon clothes.

Today's bride is not likely to be dependent on
her husband for clothes money. She'll be shopping for her own wardrobe before the wedding,
and will be concerned with the practicalities of
luggage weight limitations, easy-care fabrics, and
mix-and-match clothing that will be versatile for
a variety of activities.

Trousseau list of Sonia Keppel, married in 1920 to Robert
Cubitt, fourth son of Lord Ashcombe:

- Three dozen each of night-gowns, petticoats, bodices,
  chemises, knickers, stockings, and handkerchiefs
- a dozen pairs of evening and day shoes
- six pairs of stays
- a pink satin peignoir, trimmed with ostrich feathers
- a quilted blue velvet dressing-gown
- two evening dresses, one black velvet and one pink velvet
- two tea-gowns
- three day dresses, three afternoon dresses, and three
  tweed suits
- a traveling coat with matching hats, jerseys and skirts

The bride's going-away outfit was a dress of pale blue mar-
ocain, a black velvet coat with a gray fox collar, and a gray
cap trimmed with osprey feathers.

Ann Monsarrat,
. . . And the Bride Wore

The bride's mystique is left at the altar as a spirited young wife rides off with her husband.

Let's Take a Trip

What's an ideal honeymoon site? Seclusion, glamour, excitement, adventure, all have their lure. Many of today's new marrieds are already seasoned travelers. The honeymoon may be a chance to see something new—as with the California couple who went for one week to Hawaii, because the groom had never seen it, and one week to Barbados, because the bride had never seen that! For others, it's a chance to relax after the feverish pitch of wedding planning. The typical couple stays away about eight days, although 12 percent travel for two full weeks or more.

Over the years "in" honeymoon spots became popular, but unlike other trends, few ever faded away. The very qualities that made Niagara Falls a favorite destination in the 1930s—natural wonders, romantic settings, easy access—keep it a favorite option today. Newlyweds used to climb aboard Pullman sleepers bound for the American side of the falls; today couples prefer the Canadian side, some extending their trip north to Quebec City for sightseeing or skiing.

And speaking of the thirties, how adventurous it was to leave by motor car, bags lashed to the luggage rack, headed for Atlantic City by the sea. The boardwalk with its lights and hurly-burly beckoned honeymooners, including the famous —George Jessel, Mary Pickford. There was ocean bathing for recreation, games of chance for excitement, rolling carts for romance. They stayed at magnificent hotels that lined the boardwalk. Today Atlantic City offers new glamorous beach-front hotels with gambling casinos and classy entertainment as added attractions.

near therapeutic spas, were places where every need could be attended to. The dining was sumptuous; the dancing, elegant; the grounds, manicured. Honeymooners stayed at the Cloister (the "Shangri-la" of the South), in Sea Island, Georgia; the Homestead, in Hot Springs, Virginia; and the Greenbrier, in White Sulphur Springs, West Virginia. At the Greenbrier, newlyweds—including President and Mrs. John Tyler, Mr. and Mrs. Joseph Kennedy, and Debbie Reynolds and Eddie Fisher—had exclusive rights to stroll on "Paradise Row." In the Catskills, big resorts such as Grossinger's or the Concord rivaled each other with spectacular feasts, shows, and sporting events. And in the Poconos, now "the honeymoon capital of the world," things began quite simply with the opening of Rudolf von Hoevenberg's Farm on the Hill in 1945. Couples applied for the privilege of "practicing for life ahead" by making beds, keeping house, and waiting tables

With the advent of luxury liners, such as the *Queen Mary,* wealthier couples set sail for an extended tour of Europe. Such leisurely relaxation, with time for sightseeing, shopping, and cultural events, was very stylish.

In the forties, honeymooners cruised to Bermuda via the Furness-Withy line and stayed at the Princess, one of the old Bermudiana hotels. Hawaii-bound travelers sailed on the Matson Line for the Royal Hawaiian Hotel. Cruise lines maintained the hotels after ships were replaced by more efficient air travel.

Grand hotels, often built in lovely settings or

Honour, riches, marriage-blessing,
Long continuance, and increasing,
Hourly joys be still upon you!
Juno sings her blessings on you.

William Shakespeare,
The Tempest

In this tropical Jamaican paradise, a modern Adam and Eve enjoy a private interlude.

Honeymoon memories are made of this.

with other young marrieds—a far cry from the heart-shaped pools and pampering that couples experience in lavish Pocono resorts today!

During the fifties, tropical paradises, once open only in season (December to April), became available all year round. Honeymoon pairs headed south to Miami Beach. The Fontainebleau attracted Sammy Davis, Jr., and Mai Britt, Keely Smith and Louis Prima, Tony Martin and Cyd Charisse. Jamaica, then Puerto Rico, and gradually other Caribbean islands became the new cruise destinations. Today romantics reach even the most remote islands by air or sea.

Las Vegas, just a hop away from Los Angeles, drew a host of entertainers—Elvis Presley, Judy Garland, Ann Miller, Mickey Rooney—for quick, easy weddings. "The Little Church of the West" and "Cupid's Wedding Chapel" continue to offer a wedding with little fuss and bother in a city of glitter and gambling.

In the sixties the West Coast beckoned. Palm Springs became the genteel alternative to Las Vegas—after all, Clark Gable and Carole Lombard honeymooned there. Today the charm of San Francisco, the majesty of the Oregon coast, the rustic appeal of the Rockies, offer a variety of honeymoon experiences.

Acapulco, the original Mexican resort, attracted bright Hollywood and political personalities (such as the John F. Kennedys) to its exotic beaches. Bathers could follow the sun from the popular morning beach to the afternoon beach. Those searching for the Love Boat will find it, the *Pacific Princess*, in the sun-kissed waters of Acapulco Bay. Mexico has since created several idyllic resorts. Ixtapa and Cancun were each designed to take advantage of favorable weather, best travel routes, and abundant natural resources.

Even before F. Scott and Zelda Fitzgerald had

their infamous "champagne bath" during their Biltmore Hotel honeymoon, New York was a place where honeymooners could find constant excitement. The Plaza, the Waldorf-Astoria, the St. Regis, and other fine hotels gave honeymooners—royalty and commoners alike—the red carpet treatment. Couples, then and now, find spectacular events, beautiful surroundings, and privacy when they want it. New lavish hotels—the Helmsley Palace, the Grand Hyatt, the Vista—have opened in "the city that never sleeps." Honeymooners, of course, may choose to!

Air travel, firmly established in the sixties, changed honeymoon travel completely. Even short trips to Europe, or any place in the world, became a reasonable choice, offering excitement, history, and a wealth of enchanting places to stay.

Choice of honeymoon spot may be made according to sentiment—where the couple met or an ancestral country; or because of their love for a particular activity—skiing, scuba diving, tennis, camping, gourmet dining.

Whatever locale newlyweds choose, whether

These postcards bring lucky honeymooners' greetings from scenic spots in Italy and California.

faraway exotic or just around the corner, they must double-check reservations, tickets, traveler's checks, passports, or foreign currency if necessary. Nothing rubs the bloom off the rose faster than travel problems during a honeymoon. Couples whose plans are made long before the whirlwind of parties and wedding activities begins can take off confidently through that flurry of rice and rose petals for the time of their lives.

Newlywed Names

When the newlyweds arrive at the "honeymoon hotel," one of the first things they may have to do is to register. What name to use? The famous sometimes choose pseudonyms: Shirley Temple and her new husband signed in as Emma and Emil Glutz in 1946. The reclusive Howard Hughes and actress Jean Peters escaped notice as G. A. Johnson and Mary Ann Evans in 1957. But for most of us, press hounds are not the problem.

It is tradition, not a legal requirement, for the bride to assume her husband's name at marriage. Today many brides are keeping their own names, often because they are already known that way professionally. It is not a new issue: Lucy Stone, an early proponent of women's rights, and her husband decided together that she should keep her own name when they married in 1855. Whatever the bride decides—and most still prefer to take their husband's name—the decision should be made early enough to allow for ordering any printed stationery in good time. Cards giving a new address, enclosed in wedding invitations or announcements, may indicate the choice of names.

At Home

Susan Smith and Jesse Bickel

321 East 48th Street

New York, New York 10017

after the Seventeenth of June

Often newspaper wedding announcements mention that the bride is retaining her maiden name, when that is the case, and of course she can let friends know simply by continuing to use her name.

A time for fun and games and laughter.

After the wedding: three creative departures for a new life.

Thank-yous

When the honeymoon is over, the bride and groom return to reality—and to acknowledging the remainder of their wedding gifts. Thank-you notes used to be solely the bride's responsibility. It was her task to stock up on attractive stationery and write personal notes of thanks for all the presents, including those from the groom's relatives and friends. Today she and her groom write the notes together. The bride may acknowledge gifts they have received from her relatives and friends, while the groom acknowledges those from his family and friends. Or they may both express their thanks on the same note.

However the work is divided, it should be accomplished as soon as possible after returning home; and there is no excuse for not writing.

Presents that are received before the wedding can be acknowledged at that time. This will reduce the number of thank-you notes that have to be written after the honeymoon—and lets the sender know the gift has arrived.

While they are on their honeymoon, many couples send a note of thanks or a gift to their parents. The heartfelt sentiment is often the best gift in this case.

Anniversary Waltz

Each married couple stretches their life together on a loom and begins to weave. Threads cross and crisscross as the pattern takes shape, rich with design, bright with hope, while the weavers labor on. For marriage doesn't "just happen"; a successful union takes an investment of time, effort, and creativity. The pattern develops, made bolder

Written aboard the Mouette, *May 27th*

. . . Oh, Mother—It was so lovely. I wouldn't change one thing: the walk around the old garden (and the new garden this morning with Con); lunch (although I was too excited to eat my favorite asparagus); every single person there . . . all that lovely warm group. It was so lovely walking down the steps *with Daddy* into that group. I wouldn't change the dress, *the veil*, the flowers (that Elisabeth did so *beautifully*—columbine and larkspur), or any of it. Cutting the cake, kissing everyone! Wasn't Dr. Brown *dear*. It was all perfect. But you want to know what C. thinks: *just the same thing!*

Anne Morrow Lindbergh,
Hour of Gold, Hour of Lead

and more complex by the sharing of personal traditions with close friends and family. And when the fabric is finally complete, it is an heirloom to treasure and to pass on to others.

No couple knows, when they speak the words "for better for worse," just what the future will hold. Marking each anniversary year helps many couples hold on to the magic that inspired the pattern of their very special marriage. It may be listening to "our song," revisiting a sentimental spot, or winding an anniversary clock—the clock with the slow torsion pendulum that will run a full year without rewinding.

Niagara Falls has long been the classic honeymoon spot.

Traditional Gifts for Special Anniversary Years

First	paper
Fifth	wood
Tenth	tin, aluminum
Fifteenth	crystal
Twentieth	china
Twenty-fifth	silver
Thirtieth	pearls
Fortieth	rubies
Forty-fifth	sapphires
Fiftieth	gold
Sixtieth	diamonds

Reaffirmation of Vows

The reaffirmation of wedding vows, a religious ceremony that has become popular during the past ten years, gives every married couple, young or old, the chance to renew their pledge of lasting commitment. A reaffirmation can take place in a house of worship before the congregation, at home, or in some other meaningful spot. The celebration can be anything the couple want it to be—the fancy wedding they never had, a family reunion, or just a giant party.

Some couples reaffirm their vows when a son or daughter marries, or on an occasion that is already a joyous "gathering in of the clan," such as a religious or national holiday. The marriage ceremony in the revised *Book of Common Prayer* now contains a prayer of renewal for all married couples present at a wedding, a warm and wonderful way to share the blessing of marriage.

THE BRIDE'S MAGAZINE

WINTER 1939-1940 · FIFTY CENTS

8

The Bride: Yesterday, Today, and Tomorrow

A bride is a bride is a bride—she is both timely and timeless. Influenced by the styles and mores of her era, on her wedding day she is nevertheless unique, whether a young girl marrying for the first time or an older woman attended by her grown children. Her ceremony becomes extraordinary: it is infused with society's traditions and rites.

The bride, as the principal player in one of the most basic human dramas, has a role that communicates some truths about the times to her audience. Yet no matter how customs change, the wedding ritual still unifies the friends, relatives, and community members who witness it.

The wartime bride of the early 1940s insisted on ceremony, even if she married on a weekend furlough. By creating a little space for a real wedding in such a crazy time, she declared that she would be the caretaker of tradition while the nation was in chaos.

The barefoot bride of the late sixties and early seventies made a strong statement for both herself and her generation. She would not accept traditional ways; she would reinterpret the ceremony. She married against a background of natural beauty, to the words of Kahlil Gibran and the music of a dulcimer. She served macrobiotic wedding cake and wore her own simple homemade cotton dress. She thought of this marriage service as uniquely hers, a personal rite. But she was saying it for all the brides during those years:

Fifty years of Bride's *magazine covers reflect the changing decades.*

"I am not what you expect a bride to be; I will not be what you expect a wife to be. I am outside the timeworn conventions. I am today!"

Somewhere, right now, a bride is planning her wedding. How different will hers be from the ceremonies described in this chapter by brides from past decades? There is a thread that runs unbroken through their memoirs. No matter that America has changed dramatically since the thirties. Never mind that villages have become exurban centers; that telephones have created a vast communications network; that the Wright brothers' single-engine prop plane has led us to outer space. In spite of woman's changing role, her political clout, her awareness of her body, her status in the working world, clearly there is still that gossamer thread that links brides from generation to generation.

What is that common bond? It is not simply being a bride—the garments, the party, the money spent. These things make a difference, but they vary with personal circumstances, change from year to year, adapt to styles and trends.

And it's not the ceremony—the vows uttered, the music or setting chosen, the traditions followed. These are tied to family history and expectations, ethnic background, or religious belief.

Then what *is* that gossamer thread? It is, in part, the conviction that, as Judith Viorst says, "married is better." Each woman who makes the momentous decision to be a bride knows that marriage is basic to humanity and to society. While millions of words have been dispatched to praise or decry, extol or criticize this unique institution, no one—not even the live-in lovers of the past decade—has ever been able to invent a valid substitute.

By sharing their memories, these "decade brides" allow us a rare glimpse into their times and private worlds. Their feelings spin the thread that connects the bride of today with all those who went before her—and with those to come.

Before and After Marriage

We used to talk of so many things,
Roses and summer and golden rings,
Music and dances and books and plays,
Venice and moonlight and future days.

Now our chief subjects are food and bills,
Genevieve's measles and Johnny's ills;
New shoes for Betty, a hat for Jane,
Taxes, insurance, the mail and rain!

We used to say that Romance would stay.
We'd walk together a magic way!
Though we don't talk as in days of yore,
Strange, is it not, that I love you more?

Anne Campbell

THE THIRTIES

The depression that began in the last months of 1929 ended a dazzling period of prosperity. Many people were without jobs. It meant fewer marriages, but also fewer divorces. Some said couples were too busy making ends meet to quarrel.

Then in 1933, good news for brides! Prohibition was repealed, and once again "bubbly" could be served legally at wedding receptions.

Escapism was in the air. Young marrieds sang "Jeepers, Creepers," "I've Got Plenty of Nothing," and "Anything Goes" and rediscovered inexpensive fun and games—Monopoly, Bingo, scavenger hunts, miniature golf. By 1935, couples could afford to go out again and "hep cats" jived to Benny Goodman's swing. Uptown at the Cotton Club, Duke Ellington played "Mood Indigo" for "sophisticated ladies."

The nation's first supermarkets carried frozen foods, a real time-saver. Since most newlyweds could not afford appliances, laundromats sprang up and soon became community social centers.

In 1930 brides did not have much money for new clothes, and American designers stayed home from the Paris shows. But by 1935 the influence of Worth, Mainbocher, Rochas, Patou, and Schiaparelli (remember her "shocking pink"?) was evident in *Vogue*'s annual bridal issue and the new *So You're Going to Be Married* (later called *Bride's Magazine*). Fashion brought back bosoms and waistlines and introduced shoulder pads.

Americans were smitten with royalty, and the royal wedding news was a sensation: King Edward VIII abdicated to marry Wallis Simpson, an American divorcée and "the woman I love." Her trousseau of eighty dresses and forty hats made fascinating copy; her pale blue floor-length wedding ensemble by Mainbocher with small matching hat inspired hundreds of copies.

The song "You Must Have Been a Beautiful Baby" was a favorite of couples in 1938, the same year *Life* magazine published "Birth of a Baby," a photographic essay showing stills from a revolutionary movie of a real birth. The magazine was promptly banned in thirty-three cities. In a time of national sexual confusion, Tampax was introduced. While advice to, and advertising for,

the bride emphasized her traditional role, a few daringly original women fostered a pioneering mood: Eleanor Roosevelt (political influence); Amelia Earhart (aviation career); Marlene Dietrich (wardrobe of trousers).

Some honeymooners sailed to Europe aboard the great ocean liners—the *Queen Mary,* the *Queen Elizabeth,* the *Normandie.* The DC-3 made commercial air travel a possibility, and air-conditioned railroad cars were quite luxurious. In 1939 the New York World's Fair opened with "The World of Tomorrow" as its theme. One important innovation shown there—television—would have its commercial distribution delayed by the outbreak of war.

Wedding of Eloise Holley and Oscar Flowers, May 26, 1931, Waco, Texas

Mama met Oscar. He always said he fell in love with Mama first. We were students at Baylor University. I'd see him walking to classes and at church functions. Oh, he was handsome and very nice, but he was five years older. Then one night I had such fun with Oscar at a party—he was so jolly—we really clicked! Suddenly there was this spark . . .

By Christmas we really had a case and Oscar proposed. He asked my father if we could marry when law school finished that spring. My father said, "Wait a year and then I'll give you whatever kind of wedding you want." We were so unhappy. A year! Later we saw it was the right thing to do. Oscar had time to build us a house. I worked as a teacher. I had so much to learn—I didn't know how to cook, do laundry, or keep house. I was so naive. No one talked about sex then—not even girl friends. It's much better today. Mother talked about "a side of life with your husband that sometimes you'd rather not have to do."

When I got my ring, my mother gave an announcement tea for her lady friends and my school chums. She had ice cream molded into wedding bells sent down from Fort Worth. I had five showers, then luncheons and teas. The same people kept getting invited and had to find something to bring each time. But now when I use those things, I really do remember who gave them —such lovely things!

I don't think Mama did much else that year except work on my wedding. She sewed beautifully and always made my clothes. She made my wedding dress, even the hat, a beautiful handkerchief I carried—I still have it—and my whole trousseau. Ours was a morning wedding—it would've been too hot any other time—so you didn't wear formal. My dress was ankle length, a rose beige, almost pink, of crepe and lace. Oscar wore what he always wears when he dresses up— white shirt and black suit, tie, shoes, and Stetson.

The wedding day was beautiful and sunshiny, but hot as blixen when I walked over to our Baptist church with my father. I was real nervous. Going down the aisle he kept saying "Slow down!" The church looked so pretty—there was greenery going down the aisles and big baskets of flowers.

Four of my five bridesmaids were still at Baylor, and it was exam time for them. That's why Mama decided we should have a "come and go" reception the night *before* the wedding. She had a table decorated, and a punch bowl, and a wedding cake with rosebuds, white doves and wedding bells on it. Then, right after the wedding ceremony, the girls had to make a dash to Baylor to get back to exams.

Mother and Oscar packed his car, a blue two-door Ford, with all the breakables and a few linens. We shipped the rest. I changed to my going-away suit and looked very ladylike when we got on the road. But not for long—it was so hot and dusty. In Waco we'd seen very little effect of the Depression. But by 1931 they were starting to

feel it in the Panhandle, where we were headed. Oscar had been able to get land and build us a house by borrowing from his father.

I could hardly wait to see the house. Oscar had done it all long-distance—he sent wallpaper books and paint colors, and I'd choose what I liked. It was exactly as I'd pictured it. I thought it was the prettiest thing I had ever seen! Bit by bit, we borrowed and refinished things to furnish the house.

No one had washers. I had to soak the clothes overnight and then rub them on a scrub board. When they started help-yourself washers in town, we all went there. Not many owned an electric refrigerator. We'd ordered one that was delivered just when the wheat market dropped to twenty-seven cents a bushel. Oscar took one look at it and said, "There sits six hundred bushels of wheat." We took out the telephone, but it was too hard to do any business without it.

I tried to can—mostly to impress Oscar's mother. I never told her that during the winter, a whole bunch of jars exploded. Luckily, a Roosevelt project created a cannery nearby. You could take your produce to them—even beef and pork —and they put it in tins. We'd save up to go to Will Rogers movies. And neighbors got together about three times a week. We'd pool our hamburgers and brown beans and play cards or games. You had to make your own entertainment.

When the dust storms started, it was very frightening. We had to close up part of the house, seal the windows, and put sheets over the furniture. Finally they learned about soil conservation.

Despite the hard times, we were happy as larks in that house. A few years ago we moved to a new one. But I keep going back by—it is so filled with memories.

THE FORTIES

In the early forties life was a day-to-day affair. Personal plans had to take a back seat to national interest. Couples who had expected to arrange the wedding of their dreams suddenly found themselves making their plans around a weekend furlough. One Chicago bride flew to Kansas City with her family, expecting to spend a week before the wedding getting to know her in-laws. She arrived carrying her wedding gown in a box. Surprise! She was married right at the airport with her gown still in its box. The groom was shipping out within the next hour.

Gifts were portable so they could be easily moved from post to post. They were small, to take up as little space as possible in "duration" homes, often over garages or in basements. The War Bond was a thoughtful gift for the bridesmaids or ushers.

The war created jobs and helped solve the lingering Depression problems, but even with money, products were not available. Silk stockings were scarce, so resourceful women covered their legs with makeup and drew a seam with eyebrow pencil. Gas, food, and clothing were rationed. Women worked in new kinds of jobs, learning skills and independence at the same time. Wives assembled planes, made bullets, planted victory gardens, and served in the WACS and WAVES, so that their men could be freed for active combat.

No-nonsense clothes went with the jobs: pants became fashionable, as did man-tailored suits with broad shoulders. Hair was worn long and feminine, often in a "snood," a crocheted net. New products developed during the war would change women's lives—the electric dishwasher and frozen food meant less time in the kitchen; terylene (polyester) and nylon made washday a snap.

While the men overseas gazed longingly at Betty Grable (the Pin-Up Girl) and Rita Hayworth (the Love Goddess), the wives at home listened to Frank Sinatra croon. Sentimental songs were the favorites: "Blues in the Night,"

"As Time Goes By," and "Don't Sit Under the Apple Tree with Anyone Else but Me."

By the time the war ended, the nation was ready for a change. Christian Dior gave women a New Look—softer, fuller. Houses were snapped up as fast as they were built. The jukebox and jazz became popular. There was a return to religion. Bedsheets, in short supply during the war, appeared in colors, smart patterns, and fitted styles. It took several years for industry to catch up with the demand for cars, appliances, china, and household utensils.

Wedding of Gunvor Ohs and Cutler Tyler, November 7, 1942, Newark, New Jersey

I think to this day that we would never have married so quickly if it hadn't been for the war.

We met at the Prudential Insurance Company where we both worked. We'd been going together for a while, then a week after Pearl Harbor, Cut enlisted. In June he got a friend to buy a ring for him, got a pass, and came home to get engaged. But we still planned to be married after the war. My parents thought I was young—I was just nineteen—but they liked Cut so much. The war went on and on.

I took the bus down to visit Cut at Fort Benning, Georgia, and it looked like he would be there for a long time, training new officers. We used to listen to "I Don't Want to Walk Without You Baby" and feel so lonely. And we thought, why not be together? Why not get married? So he applied for a furlough.

It was a mad rush. I had to plan the whole wedding in two weeks! I shopped for my gown in such a hurry. It was off-white satin and had a short train and cost sixty dollars—a lot of money then. But I loved it. I shopped for my mother's dress and went for the marriage license all by myself. Cut mailed me his blood tests. But by then they were used to that at City Hall.

I had three surprise showers in those two weeks. The gifts we got then and at the wedding were very practical—blankets, linens, silverplate,

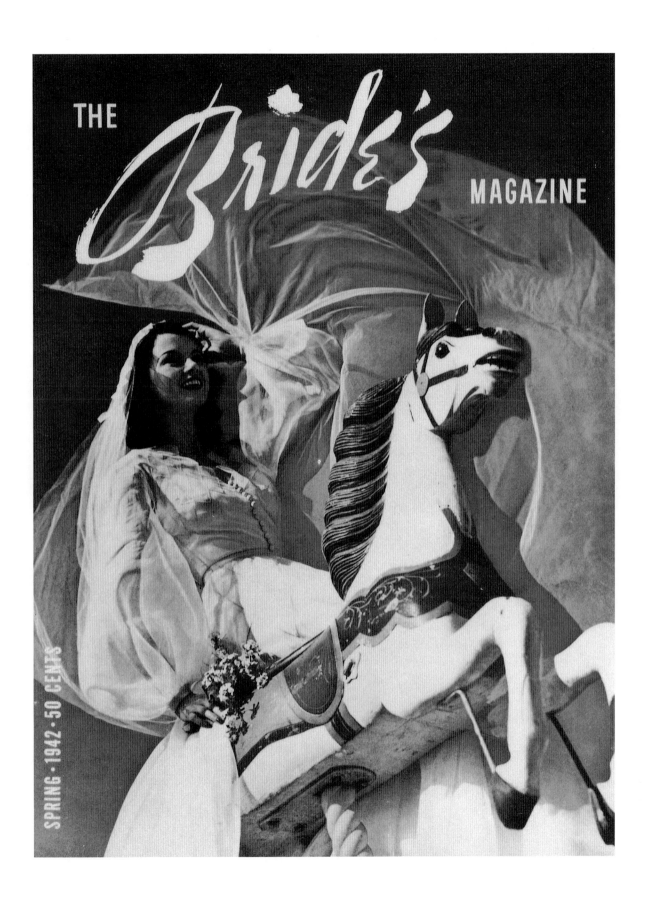

and mostly money—but I didn't bring one wedding gift with me to Georgia. It all sat in my parents' attic until after the war.

Everybody helped out. A friend lent my bridesmaid a rust-colored dress that she'd worn at another wedding. I borrowed my veil. We had the reception at home. It was a small five-room flat and jammed with people. My mother and her sisters prepared all the food—salads, sandwiches, punch. My mother had been saving ration coupons and she had mine—no problem getting butter and sugar. We were strict Swedish Baptists so there was no liquor at the reception and no dancing. But it was fun. The bakery made the cake—fruitcake was what you had then. It was three tiers with a little bride and groom on the top. I still have them.

The wedding was in our Swedish Baptist church, and Cut's Presbyterian minister helped with the service. It was old-fashioned, and I remember saying "obey." I felt sad on the way to the church because my father was sick. I wasn't sure he could make it down the aisle with me, but

he did. I guess that kept me from being nervous about myself. I can still see Cut standing at the front of the church with his best man. He was wearing his uniform because in wartime, if you were in the service, you couldn't go out in anything but your uniform.

Weddings were family affairs then, so there were lots of kids. Some of my friends from work were there, but most of Cut's were in the service. A friend of Cut's played the piano—there was no organ—and someone, I can't remember who, sang, "I Love You Truly." It rained that day . . . someone told me that was good luck. It was a very nice wedding, but getting married was the important thing. There were too many serious things happening in the world to worry about wedding details.

I was so excited at the reception, I didn't eat a thing. Then we drove to New York for a three-day honeymoon, and the first thing I wanted to do was get a hamburger. After our honeymoon, we sold the car. We couldn't get gas for it. We took a train to Georgia and lived off-base in a

room in someone's house. We really had a very happy time there. Then everything changed. They broke up the unit. Cut got sent overseas and I went home to live with my parents. I really thought I might never see Cut again. He had gone to the end of the world. Every day I'd come home from work and say, "Did I get any mail?" Sometimes there would be ten letters at one time —V-letters, photocopies with things censored out. Some days there would be none. We wrote to each other every day, but still we felt so out of touch.

My father had asked us not to have children, just in case Cut went overseas and did not come back. He didn't want me left with a fatherless child. We didn't want children then either—no one knew what would happen.

At last the war was over. Cut phoned when he landed at Fort Dix and said he was coming home. I was walking down the hill to meet the trolley when I saw this soldier walking up the hill. I started running. He started running. He looked so good. I'll never forget that moment.

THE FIFTIES

After the emotional scars of the war years, the nation yearned for peace and prosperity. Americans were spending—some with the new credit cards. Goods poured from the horn of plenty to meet the demand. Newlyweds pursued the American dream, saving for the colonial, split-level, or ranch-style home in the suburbs with a two-car garage. Interiors were "easy-care"; furniture, Early American or Danish Modern; the television —now color or portable—would occupy a prominent place in the living room. The bride's gifts might include an electric frying pan, an electric can opener, and a four-slice toaster. Energy was cheap. Women attended Tupperware Home Parties to buy the popular plastic products.

Dr. Benjamin Spock's permissive style of parenting popularized in *Baby and Child Care* (1946) was the new creed of a child-centered nation. Games, books, and toys tailored for tots were a big market. Walt Disney's *King of the Wild Frontier* set off a Davy Crockett madness. Parents

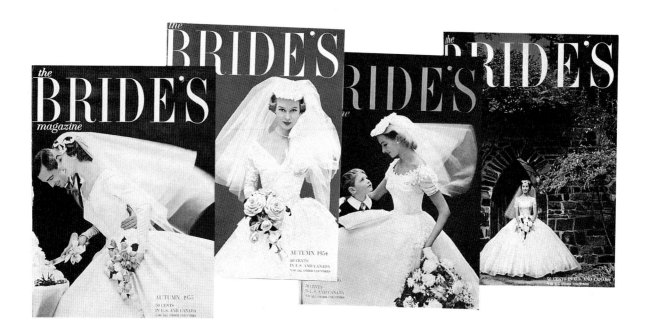

spent $100 million on movie-related goods.

In 1954 *McCall's* coined the word "together-ness" to describe the family turned inward on itself. Games like Scrabble encouraged the family to play together; Billy Graham, Norman Vincent Peale, and Bishop Fulton Sheen helped them pray together.

Chevys with fins, "T-birds" with whitewalls, "Studeys," convertibles, station wagons—cars changed the lifestyle. Signs of the times were Holiday Inns, drive-in bank windows, shopping centers, McDonald's, drive-in movies, and car coats.

In 1950 young people ended the evening with "Goodnight, Irene," but by 1955 rock and roll substituted "Rock Around the Clock." Teenag-ers became a distinct market with their own styles (crinolines, circle pins, bobby socks, crew cuts); slang ("are you for real?" "catch some rays," "fruit boots," "blotto," "out to lunch"); and idols (Dick Clark, Elvis Presley, Fabian, and Frankie Avalon). Teenage romance was serious. Boys and girls "went steady." Lowering the mar-

---

A Lifelong Struggle

When you have married your wife, you would think you were got upon a hill-top, and might begin to go downward by an easy slope. But you have only ended courting to begin marriage. Falling in love and winning love are often difficult tasks to overbearing and rebellious spirits; but to keep in love is also a business of some importance, to which both man and wife must bring kindness and goodwill. The true love-story commences at the altar, when there lies before the married pair a most beautiful contest of wisdom and gener-osity, and a life-long struggle towards an unattainable ideal, ay, surely unattainable, from the very fact that they are two instead of one.

Robert Louis Stevenson

riage age prompted articles like "Why They Can't Wait to Wed" in *Parents*. Whether because of sexual precocity, insecurity about the world, or availability of jobs, by 1960 one of every four eighteen-year-olds was married. Worthwhile goals for a young woman: be desirable as a bride, successful as a wife and mother, capable as a hostess.

Conformity was comforting to the Silent Generation that pushed the threat of "The Bomb" out of sight. People sought refuge in tranquilizers and bomb shelters. Excitement was often vicarious; gossip columnists thrived on movie-star tattle. Meanwhile the Beats fought collectivity with individualism, and books and movies searched for values amidst intellectual and moral chaos: Jack Kerouac's *On the Road*, J. D. Salinger's *Catcher in the Rye*, and James Dean's *The Wild Ones* wove their points of view into the fabric of American thinking.

Wedding of
Brenda Weiss to J. Ronald Moskowitz
June 15, 1958, Cleveland, Ohio

Our dating years were my high-school years. It was partying, studying, good times, the prom—nothing very heavy. Friday nights there were house parties with a group of kids we hung around with. We'd go to movies or listen to music —I loved all kinds of music—the slow songs, rock and roll, whatever came through the radio. And we danced.

Ron and I were going steady when I was a senior in high school. He was in his second year of college. I wore his pendant from AZA, an organization for Jewish young men. The youth group at our temple was our social life. We first met there—bowling. It never crossed my mind to date anyone but Jewish boys. It was just an expectation that I grew up with. Ron had a great personality, good looks, intelligence. We went to each other's home for dinner. Our backgrounds were the same, so there were no major conflicts. It was all very natural.

Graduation night, Ron came to drive me to the high school. I was wearing my cap and gown. He gave me this little box—a graduation gift. It was an engagement ring. Everyone knew we were serious—we'd dated for three years—so it was a foregone conclusion that we'd end up getting married. Of course I wore the ring that night to graduation. That was exciting. Walking up for my diploma, I heard, "Let's see the ring," so I'd kind of turn my hand so people could see it.

We were engaged for a year. My mother and I had a wonderful time planning the wedding. I was the only daughter and we were very close. Whatever I wanted was what my parents wanted me to have. It was important to me that it be a big beautiful wedding. I knew it was a major step in my life and I wanted something special to remember. I guess I grew up looking at bridal magazines. Being a bride was something to look forward to.

I woke up on my wedding day with a case of nerves. I was sure about Ron—I guess I was thinking about getting married, the future, what it would be like. The wedding wasn't until evening. At last there was something to do—we all went to the beauty shop—and then I calmed down. We were to be married at the Temple on the Heights and that's where I dressed. Mine was an exquisite gown, with a very full skirt and an overlay of lace panels. The sleeves and the bodice

AUTUMN 1958

50 CENTS
IN U.S. AND CANADA
$1.00 ALL OTHER COUNTRIES

were lace. I wore a crown with a tulle veil. The grandmothers, bridesmaids, my mother-in-law, all came in to see me.

While we were getting ready for the procession, Ron's cousin, a cantor, sang "Because." It all looked so beautiful—my mother and I both love flowers and there were flowers everywhere. The ushers were in white jackets, formal black pants, and yarmulkes; the bridesmaids were in pink, my favorite color. The organ started playing "Here Comes the Bride." The attendants went down the aisle, and then our grandparents, the parents, a flower girl, and my father and I. It was so exciting coming in. You're the star of the show! Everybody comes to help you celebrate. I saw so many friends—some smiling, waving, winking. At the pulpit, my father kissed me. That was a sentimental moment, we were both a little choked up—and then he handed me to Ron and Ron took over.

We were married under a gorgeous huppah. My mom had the florist make one. A center pole was entwined with flowers and then a canopy of flow-ers spread overhead above the rabbi and us. The service was in Hebrew, very solemn and very beautiful. The ketubbah, the marriage contract, was read in Hebrew and then in English and we both signed it. Our vows were traditional. The rabbi blessed the wine and the goblet passed to Ron, then to me, two times. Ron put the glass, wrapped in a cloth, under his foot and stomped on it. It was a symbol of joy and sorrow, but it also meant you were really married. That was a happy moment! People shouted out "Mazel tov" and "Congratulations." Ron kissed me, and as we turned to leave I thought, "Now our life together begins."

The reception was everything I could have wanted. We had a long receiving line—there were three hundred and fifty there—so they brought me a stool to lean against. But I was wearing a petticoat with a hoop in it and I had to keep positioning the skirt so the hoop wouldn't pop up.

We love to dance. The band played some of the old favorites like the "Anniversary Waltz" and some of the popular songs of the day. People were also doing the jitterbug and the Jewish folk dances like the horah, but I never liked to see a bride pick up her voluminous dress to do those lively dances. I stayed away from them. Friends kept asking, "Why don't you sneak out early?" But it was my wedding. I knew I'd only have one. I wanted to stay and enjoy it. So we stayed to the end. It was a very exceptional day.

For our honeymoon we drove up to the Concord in the Catskills. We didn't want a strictly "newlywed" place and the Concord was special to Ron. His family vacationed there. We could just blend in—I think I'd have died if they'd introduced us as newlyweds.

We lived in an apartment for a year before moving to a house, and we've lived in Cleveland ever since. I worked very briefly. Ron didn't want me to work and I was agreeable. Most people then thought that the wife shouldn't work unless she absolutely had to. Beatniks, the Korean War— those things seemed very far away. They just didn't figure into our lives. My world was very nice. It was taking care of the apartment, preparing the meals, visiting friends and our families, and getting used to being married. It was all new. The families were there for moral support—every Friday night we went to Ron's parents' for the traditional Friday night observance and dinner. I always felt I was helping Ron do what he was trying to do. We were conserving money, saving for the future—for the children. We had a baby a year and a half later. Everything was adequate.

I know that nowadays women think differently, but for me raising children was a marvelous accomplishment. And I felt that my being there, at home, was an important contribution.

This year my son married, we celebrated our twenty-fifth anniversary, and my parents, their fiftieth—all happy occasions and times to reflect. I love having the photographs of all the weddings. They bring back so many memories. I feel very lucky. When I married I was only eighteen, but it seemed quite a natural thing to do. If I had it to do over again, I would do it the same way. Being a wife and mother was exactly what I wanted to do with my life.

THE SIXTIES

The Bob Dylan song "The Times They Are A-Changing" said it all. Values and styles were being tested all over the world. Young people raised questions about family structure, religion, government, the military, education, business, the environment, the sexes, and civil rights. A new vocabulary emerged.

"Women's Lib." The enormous response of women to Betty Friedan's seminal book *The Feminine Mystique,* and later to *Ms.* magazine, showed that feminism was an idea whose time had come. Women broke out of their little boxes and began defying traditional expectations. A bride-to-be might have danced to "Love Makes the World Go Round" in 1961 wearing a bouffant hairdo and a turtleneck sweater. But by 1969 she would be planning to marry in miniskirt and love beads to the strains of "Aquarius" from *Hair.* Tradition was suspect. Living together became a defiant alternative to marriage. Many newlyweds felt confused. Divorce rates soared.

"Free love" . . . "the pill." Masters and Johnson published *Human Sexual Response* in 1966.

Its message: sexual problems can be corrected if both partners in the marriage are treated. No longer could the "frigid wife" or "impotent husband" be solely responsible. Sexual fulfillment became a two-way street. Being married didn't have to mean being parents. The oral contraceptive tablet won immediate acceptance from women but set off controversies about moral and social values. The fertility pill made pregnancy possible for other couples. When the bride did become pregnant, amniocentesis could detect problems in the embryo, could even foretell the infant's sex; the rubella vaccine prevented German measles—related deformities; and disposable diapers made baby care easier.

"Black power" . . . "black is beautiful." The slogans heralded the new status of a disadvantaged race and a change in national awareness. But awareness did not come easily: the Watts riots, civil rights marches, school desegregation battles, the assassination of Martin Luther King. The movie *Guess Who's Coming to Dinner* portrayed the human feelings of families learning to live with a new social order that included interracial marriage.

"The boob tube" . . . "media." Television homogenized the nation. In 1965 alone, 11 million television sets were purchased. TV brought the Kennedy-Nixon debates, the nighttime soap opera *Peyton Place*, situation comedies, game shows, family entertainment, the news, and celebrity weddings. Some notable couples: Elizabeth Taylor and Richard Burton; Princess Anne-Marie of Denmark and King Constantine of Greece; Princess Margaret and Anthony Armstrong-Jones; Hope Cooke and the King of Sikkim; while on the *Johnny Carson Show*, Miss Vicky and Tiny Tim said their vows before an audience of millions. Three presidential daughters were married in a swirl of publicity—Luci Johnson, Lynda Bird Johnson, and Tricia Nixon. And one former First Lady—Jacqueline Kennedy—wed Aristotle Onassis on his very own Greek island. The Telstar communication satellite made European telecasts possible. The world began to shrink.

the
BRIDE'S
magazine

AUTUMN 1961 / 50 CENTS

**WEDDING
FASHIONS**
The newest
and best

YOUR HOME
Everything
needed in
Silver
China
Glass
Linens
Furniture
Carpets
Gifts

**BERMUDA
HONEYMOON**
A complete guide

Special feature
**THE COST
OF GETTING MARRIED**
and who pays for what

"Mission control" . . . "transplants." Astronaut John Glenn orbited the earth in 1962; Neil Armstrong walked on the moon in 1969. Self-sustaining colonies spinning between the earth and moon became real possibilities, not figments of a science-fiction writer's imagination. The new technology brought digital clocks, artificial limbs, electronic pacemakers. Christiaan Barnard performed the first heart transplant. Zip codes made automated mail possible.

"Flower children" . . . "hippies" . . . "tripping" . . . "psychedelic." The idealism inspired by John F. Kennedy gave way to anguished protest after his assassination. Rock and folk singers became the philosophers for the counterculture —the Beatles, Rolling Stones, Peter, Paul, and Mary, delivered the message. Styles went from mini to maxi to unisex. The "twist" was the rage at the Peppermint Lounge in New York City. Bodies contorted to the "frug," "monkey," and the "bossa nova." Many young people, confused about what was happening to their world, turned to drugs.

Wedding of Elinor Casey and Robert King, October 6, 1968, Bronx, New York

Our wedding at Our Lady of Mercy was a celebration of what we had chosen to do. People could either approve or disapprove. That was their problem.

Robert and his friends had crashed my eighteenth-birthday party. We knew each other from the Civil Air Patrol, a youth group we all belonged to, but I was in the Bronx group and he was in Manhattan. We were plain old friends—consoling each other when our current loves failed us—for about five years.

Robert is black West Indian and I am Irish Catholic. Our friends from C.A.P. were very relaxed about interracial dating. It wasn't an issue for us. We both dated many people. Outside C.A.P. it was another story. I grew up in a neighborhood where an Irish Catholic dating an Italian Catholic was considered newsworthy. So if you went any further than that it was really serious business. Robert called me to talk about his prob-

lems with a soured romance and said, "Hey, why don't we do something we've never done before; why don't *we* go out?" We went to *Camelot,* a very romantic movie. That was in March. On August sixth, his birthday, Robert announced that we were getting married. I hadn't expected him to pop an "announcement" instead of a question. He said, "Oh, oh, I guess I've done this wrong," and got down on his knees for another try. "Will you please marry me on October sixth?" He forgets everything but his own birthday, so he wanted a date he could remember. And he has! The songs from *Camelot* became very special to us. We play them on every anniversary.

My father had been giving me a hard time about a boy I had been dating who happened to be a white Roman Catholic with long hair and a motorcycle. He called him a "hippie" and a "weirdo." But when I got engaged to Robert he said, "Whatever happened to that nice young man with the motorcycle?" But whatever I might do, I was still his child. He was very sick by the time of our wedding; in fact he died two months

later. The night before the wedding, he said to Robert, "I trust you'll take good care of my daughter. My daughter and my wife tell me you are a good man, and I'm assuming you know how to be a husband now that my daughter's going to be your wife." It was his blessing. I was very grateful. I would have liked to really talk it out, but he was much too weak; he couldn't even come to the wedding. Some may have thought he was boycotting it. But I knew he wasn't, and that's all that mattered.

I'm sure my mother would have been happier if I'd married someone white. But she made me feel the choice was mine and if I thought I'd be happier with Robert than with someone else, then she'd be there for me. She always has been.

Robert's family was very accepting. When someone asked his mother why he hadn't picked a nice West Indian girl, she said, "Because he picked someone he loved."

We had an unpleasant experience at the wedding rehearsal. The priest—a young Irishman—took me aside and said, "You didn't tell me your intended groom was black." I said I hadn't seen that question on the church's form. "Well, I don't think it's legal," he replied. I just told him it was 1968, this wasn't the South, and it certainly was legal.

When I think about my wedding, I remember an unbelievable series of crises. They're funny now, but at the time I sure wondered what was going on.

The printer told me he'd lost the invitations. I went down there and camped out in his office until he found them.

It was Friday afternoon before we got to the Marriage License Bureau. The lady said sorry, but they close early on Fridays. "Oh no, you don't understand, we're getting married on Sunday, and you're not closed." We got the license, but it took a while.

Then the flowers. When they arrived, my wedding bouquet was plastic! I got on the telephone. They said the lilies of the valley and freesias I'd ordered were out of season. I ran out and got myself a bouquet—white roses and chrysanthemums—and sued them later.

My brother walked me down the aisle, his hand in a cast with thirteen stitches—he had cut himself very badly helping us move into our apartment the night before the wedding.

My sister missed the rehearsal, so when I went to hand her my flowers she said, "I've already got flowers."

When the priest sprinkled the holy water, Robert wasn't expecting it. We were up on a step and he almost fell backwards. Then he said, "Watch the suit, it's rented." We all started laughing, even the priest.

My mother wanted us to have as nice a wedding as possible. I didn't want to burden them unduly,

so we decided on a relatively small but very traditional wedding. I chose Our Lady of Mercy Church, because anything of any religious significance had happened to me in that church. It was an eclectic wedding party. Robert's Episcopalian. His best man was Jewish. My sister and I were Catholic. We kind of laughed our way through the service.

We rode in a limousine. It was a very exciting day for me. I just felt good. My dress was floor-length, very plain white satin, fitted to the waist, and then almost an A-line. It had a mandarin collar and tatting at the cuffs. The veil was full-length and attached to a crown. I would love to have saved it, but I lent it to a friend who moved away, and I never got it back. I wore a borrowed garter with blue ribbons.

It was all very beautiful. My mother looked wonderful. I was twenty-four and the first of her children to marry. She was pleased. About two hundred people came to the church. We had the receiving line at the back of the church, and I remember feeling very pleased and gratified that so many people came.

Robert's sister had a reception for eighty people at her apartment on Riverside Drive. It had a gorgeous view of Manhattan and the George Washington Bridge. I went over the day before and helped her do the windows, polish the furniture, and everything. She had background music and pretty flowers (real ones!), champagne, caviar, cheese, crackers, and a traditional wedding cake with a little *white* bride and groom. That was funny. The bakery had white couples or black couples, but no mixed ones. Robert didn't care if it looked like him or like me. (Recently I showed it to my daughters. The younger one said, "But it doesn't look like Daddy." The other one said,

"That's all right; it doesn't look like Mommy either.")

I had a wonderful time at the party. I met many of Robert's relatives for the first time. It was a very mixed group of people all enjoying each other. I didn't have much champagne—I was high on the day. We stayed and had another piece of cake and coffee, then went home, changed, and went out shopping for breakfast fixings. We took a couple of days off from work to relax, do some shopping, and work on the apartment.

I married Robert because of who he is as a human being, not because of his skin color. I've known some people whose marriage was "a cause." I think that's unfair. It's very enriching for our children and for us to have two different traditions to celebrate and think about. And it's fun. We make a big thing of St. Patrick's Day and West Indian Day so they understand their roots on both sides.

I never anticipated having any problems with Robert based on color. Any difficulties have not stemmed from our races or different cultural backgrounds, but from our individual personalities. And always, if we start talking about our wedding, the energy, good feelings, and amusement come right back. We continue to treasure the magic of that day.

THE SEVENTIES

In the course of this decade, American values were both confused and confirmed. The confusion was typified by the kidnapping of a young, wealthy socialite, Patti Hearst. When she was pictured in the media participating in her captors' criminal acts, it appeared she also espoused their terrorist philosophy. If that could happen, anything could. And did.

Americans learned they were not totally self-sufficient: their automobiles stood in long gas lines thanks to the Arab oil boycott. Their sense of national virtue was seriously undermined when President Richard Nixon resigned after the Wa-

tergate scandal was uncovered. Their affluence was threatened when inflation nearly bankrupted New York City in 1975 and forced many newlyweds to live with parents instead of in a home of their own.

But many of the old values were confirmed, also exemplified by Patti Hearst. Several years after her surrender and trial, she married, had a child, and settled down to a conventional life. The heiress was not the only bride to seek a traditional wedding. There was a revival of the large, old-fashioned wedding. In 1976 the United States celebrated its bicentennial. Nostalgia, antiques, and Americana were popular. The television mini-series *Roots* sent people searching for their own origins, and ethnic customs and dances were woven into many weddings. Tracing the family history gave couples a sense of continuity.

Perception of the family changed as traditional wife/husband roles became obsolete. In 1977 statistics showed that only 15.9 percent of all households included a father as sole wage earner, a mother as full-time homemaker, and at least one child. Other households might consist of a single parent and offspring, a couple childless by choice, the "blended" family of the divorced and remarried, a "gay" marriage, a two-salaried family. The discovery of DNA, the human genetic code, raised ethical questions about human reproduction—should genes be altered? The first "test tube" baby was born in 1978.

In the seventies, women became firmly established in the marketplace, more and more of them entering fields once predominantly masculine such as construction, medicine, the ministry, law, politics. Two feminist issues, abortion and the Equal Rights Amendment, gained ground and set off a feverish backlash among traditionalists.

It was called the "Me Decade," with a personal, rather than a collective, effort to "get your head together." There was a narcissistic quality to the pursuit of personal awareness and fulfillment. Physical fitness became a credo. Joggers were everywhere in fashion-coordinated sweatsuits. Diet, pure foods, appearance, were very important. Designers whose discreet labels used to be hidden inside their clothing put their names boldly on the outside of garments. The search for meaning and values led Americans to Eastern religions, tarot cards and astrology, and cults.

Science grew more familiar as computers, space travel, "Star Wars," and microwaves entered the home. The silicon chip made hand-held calculators, home computers, video games, and video player/tape recorders possible. "Instant replay" was a way to slow down and make sense of fast-breaking events. But science also made the preservation of the environment a world-wide issue. Technology rapidly depleted the resources shared by all. There were campaigns to conserve, recycle, encourage solar power, save the whales.

Everything went faster in the seventies. The Metroliner, a high-velocity train, and the Concorde, a supersonic passenger aircraft, both sped up travel. Successful people "moved in the fast lane." Popular music—rock and disco—accompanied a lifestyle where rhythm was more important than lyrics. By decade's end, Americans were ready to slow down the stressful pace, and a back-to-basics movement began.

Wedding of Anne Willett and John Dawson,
August 19, 1973
Sanbornville, New Hampshire

John and I both summered in New Hampshire. My aunt wanted me to meet this really neat guy, a golfer. So I got out there on the course and didn't even know which end of the club to hold. I was very attracted to John—he's muscular, blue-eyed, tall, and blond—his hair was long then. He was a hippie—very mellow—and I was

kind of hyper. We've completely reversed roles now! We really hit it off. By the second date we were talking marriage.

But then summer was over and he went back to Columbia University in New York. I was working and lived with my parents in Massachusetts. I was very young, very naive, very into my family. He was the first guy I ever took an interest in. I was the eldest, so this was my parents' first experience with their children's courting. They were very straight. He'd come up for weekends and have to sleep at a neighbor's house—two singles couldn't sleep in the same house. So we'd do things with the family and hope the parents would go to bed early.

Then he decided to go to graduate school in California. He wanted me to come along—without vows—but at that time I couldn't do that. Now, though, I'd recommend it to my young sister or a daughter if I had one. It turned into a long-distance romance, and that wasn't good. After a while, I wrote and said, "Look . . . this isn't going to work out. You're in California and I'm in Massachusetts. Maybe you should find something else to take up your time." On spring break he invited me down to his parents' home in New Jersey. I was really nervous. I felt like this was either going to be the end or the beginning of something. He took me into his father's study and sat me down in the big desk chair. Then he got down on his knees and popped a couple of diamonds at me. I guess he threw everything he believed in aside to do that because he knew I needed that kind of proposal. Within ten minutes, I was on the phone screaming, "Mom, guess what!"

Right from the start, we knew it had to be outdoors on a mountain in New Hampshire. We

knew it would feel very open—almost naked—and we wanted to be out there in front of the whole world. We wanted the place to say, "We think this is a spot where God surpassed himself and we want to share it with you." My aunt—the matchmaker—suggested a meadow up on Cotton Mountain. We looked at it, and at each other, and knew—"this is it!"

It was a beautiful day for a wedding. I had made invitations and maps by hand. We invited everybody—first-grade teachers, high-school friends, the five-year-olds I was teaching, relatives we'd never met. They came from all over, 243 people from babies right up to ninety-year-olds. It was so much fun—warm and close—just like a very first family reunion for me. We rounded up seven four-wheel-drive trucks and ferried everyone up the hill. We even trucked up a piano and violinist.

Dad and I walked up the hill hand-in-hand. I was in the dress I'd made of homespun cotton and Belgian lace. Dad said things like, "Now if you ever have any problems you can call us; you can't come home, but you can call." My brides-

maids were wearing dresses I'd made too. And John was in his new white linen suit.

Well, I can't do anything straight. When we came around the bend they played, "Climb Every Mountain," and for our processional everyone sang, "She'll Be Comin' Round the Mountain When She Comes." We did it with lots of humor. Everyone was excited, laughing and having fun. My mother and father gave me away and John's gave him away. We tried to involve everyone in reading or singing or clapping. We were both Methodist and actually got married in the faith. We wrote our own vows together about thirty minutes before the service. Basically we promised to be honest and open with each other, and if we couldn't . . . we'd never live a lie. After the kiss, John just scooped me up and ran the rest of the way up the hill. Everyone clapped and cheered. No tears. It was all so right.

The reception was back at my uncle's house. There was a big wedding cake—chocolate with mocha frosting—but it did have flowers and a little bride and groom on top. We had a band

from town set up by the swimming pool. Some people swam and some danced. Even Grandpa got up and danced. It was a great party, and we were the last ones to leave.

I was kind of surprised by some strong emotions when it was all over. I guess it just hit me that we were leaving for California in the VW bus and I'd never lived away from home before. It was a serious cut from everything I'd ever known and it was all happening in one day. But I was on a real high then.

Our wedding structured our whole relationship. We did everything together—decided what to wear, wrote our vows, paid for it, planned it. We wanted it spontaneous and we wanted friends there to share it. It was a real strong in-love situation and that's carried us through the good times and the bad. I guess you could say our vows have continued through our whole married life.

Everybody remembers our wedding. People say it was the most warm, beautiful, exciting wedding they've ever been to. We feel just the same. I'd love to do it all over again tomorrow!

THE EIGHTIES AND BEYOND

It is no coincidence that "tradition" has reentered the bride's vocabulary after the fragmented "me"-centered seventies created a need for stability and "us." In a world that is being rapidly transformed by technological breakthroughs, the bride, that symbol of continuity, reassures us that the fundamentals remain unchanged.

In the eighties and beyond there are new things coming, but they won't necessarily drive out the old.

Courtship and entertaining will more and more take place at home—either her place or his, since fewer young men and women live with their parents now. To take in a movie, the couple can remain in their own living room with home video, cable, or pay TV to choose from.

A dinner date will mean gourmet take-out food served at home by candlelight to the romantic background music of their choice on the tape deck. Food will be geared to the international palate since everyone will travel. And new foods —high-protein wonder crops grown above ground with nutrient sprays, controlled farming of lobsters and shrimp for an insatiable market— will grace the table.

Shopping for the wedding and new home will be done through direct-mail catalogues and cable TV, both keyed by marketing computers to the special interests of the bride-to-be.

Space will be a luxury and most newlywed homes will have to be smaller, but multi-use environments and furniture will make a virtue of necessity—living will be more compact and convenient, home care a relative cinch.

In the home of the eighties and beyond, the computer will rule. Before the end of 1990, 30 million families are expected to own home computers. They will use them to pay bills, do their banking, get information on weather, traffic, stocks, shopping specials. A phone call from one's office will instruct the computer to activate the microwave oven, washing machine, dishwasher, air conditioner, thermostat, answer the phone, or set the security system.

Transportation will be so rapid that long-distance courtships—and even marriages—will pose fewer problems. A train that can travel 300 miles per hour by magnetic levitation (MAGLEV) has

already been tested in the United States and Japan. It would be capable of making the New York–Washington run in thirty minutes. Even more remarkable are the Very High Speed Transit Vehicles now being developed by researchers. These subwaylike cars will ride on electromagnetic waves in tunnels deep in the earth. Imagine New York to Los Angeles in twenty-one minutes!

Work will attract more and more women. Although hours will be shorter and more flexible, the work will be routine—much of it handling machines. Since such work is sedentary, leisure-time pursuits will have to be physical.

But in this brave new world, love will still have its day—and night. Health professionals, besides finding cures for some of our most baffling diseases, expect to discover a superlative chemical aphrodisiac. One of the new contraceptives will be a nasal spray. Many young couples will delay pregnancy while maintaining the benefits of prime-of-life conception; for them it will be possible to conceive a healthy embryo, have it frozen

and then implanted later. Other family-related miracles-to-be include choosing the sex of a baby and "mapping" genes in utero to allow intervention for abnormalities.

There will be fewer births, but people will live longer because many diseases will be conquered and the effects of growing old will be held at bay with anti-aging pills. Society will gradually grow older; by 2030 one of every five persons will be over sixty-five—but few will look it! What possibilities for enduring romance!

Wedding of
Molly Bowman and Walt Kalin,
December 20, 1982, Portland, Oregon

I'd already learned a lot about myself. Then I found somebody who enhanced my life. He made what I already had better!

I had been divorced for six years. I was almost forty, with a daughter fourteen and a son seventeen. During those single years, I came to the

conclusion that I could be happy, very comfortable, being single the rest of my life. Yet I think I always knew what kind of person could make me change my mind.

When Walt asked me what I was looking for, I knew exactly. I wanted a man who looked forty, not someone trying to look like a young macho; someone divorced, who knew what marriage is like and the pain of divorce; someone who had teenage kids, so he would understand mine; and what I really wanted was somebody who would get up on a Sunday morning and go outside with me and watch the tomatoes grow.

Walt liked that. I think he was looking for some of those same things. He was forty-two, recently separated when we met, and had three girls, twelve, seventeen, and a married twenty-year-old.

We met in May at a party at my house. I'd been giving "singles" parties with some friends— we all found it hard to meet new people. Everyone brought along someone nice. Walt and I got along real well. By our third date, we had planned a picnic with all the kids. By the time we married, they knew one another pretty well.

Walt is a very romantic man. He really did come right out and ask me those wonderful words, "Will you marry me?" That was August, and in September he moved in. I wasn't going to live with someone I hadn't decided to marry. My kids adjusted to Walt very quickly. They thought he was wonderful and they were ready for me to marry. They weren't even surprised. They seemed to know that this one was different.

I think that the time was valuable to everyone in different ways. When the wedding planning started, my son was taking a marriage and the family course at high school, dealing with reasons to marry. He asked us what made us decide to get married—why didn't we just go on living together? And so I answered that you get to a point where you want to make that commitment to each other. It seemed to make sense to him.

Walt's kids live with their mother about twenty minutes away, and they visit us. It was unfortunate that his divorce and the beginning of our relationship overlapped, because all these things that take a long time to work out just got telescoped into a concentrated period of time. Walt and his children are still working out of a divorce and into a remarriage.

At first, we were going to wait until March to marry. Then we started planning my fortieth birthday party for December 20 and thought, well, why not make it a wedding? We wanted to have it in a church, because it was a spiritual commitment. I went to my Episcopal church, where I was married the first time, and was flat out refused. The minister was very judgmental and it really was upsetting. Then we looked at church substitutes—the rented chapel, the park. Finally we met another Episcopal minister, a fantastic man, who took time to explain the church's position. He listened, told us what we'd have to do, and agreed to marry us.

Planning a second wedding is just different. Some things are more complicated—like, "Do I change my name again?" The first time I was very young, idealistic, more scared. This time I felt more in control, surer of what I was doing. The showy things—the perfect white wedding dress, the big church wedding, the right music—didn't matter. The people involved mattered, and we had to take them into consideration. When you remarry and have children, you're not just marrying each other, you're taking on the kids. We were creating a unit of ourselves and five children. We wanted to make the ceremony special for all of us, to show that even though we were not all going to be living together, we would somehow become a family that day.

So the procession was very simple—just the five kids, and my father escorting me. At the altar, Walt's kids lined up with him, and my two

with me. The basic Episcopal service was just fine for us. There were about twenty people in the congregation, just the immediate relatives.

We decided it would be impractical to buy matching dresses for the girls—they were such different ages. So we helped each one buy a dress that she felt comfortable in and would wear later. I bought a cream-colored chiffon dress with long sleeves and a little bit of ruffle, a short, cocktail type—weddingish, but not a wedding—dress. I carried a single white rose. The ceremony was very simple, a basic emotional experience. We didn't have music—just ourselves.

It crossed my mind that at my first wedding, everyone told me it was bad luck if you saw the groom on your wedding day. And there we were, five kids and two adults trying to get dressed for a wedding in one house—everybody running around, looking for missing socks and things. It was pretty funny. Walt and I were still functioning as parents, even while we were getting ready for our wedding.

We went to leave for the church and there was this big black limousine sitting outside. The kids knew we would be much too practical to spring for one. So they had decided to chip in and do it together—it was their surprise. They piled into the cars behind us and off we went to the church. After the ceremony they escorted us out to the limousine, and on the seat was a bottle of champagne and two champagne glasses. We arrived at the reception at the Waverly Country Club in great style. When the chauffeur opened the door, there were all these twinkly Christmas lights on the trees and Duncan MacKenzie in his Scottish kilt with his bagpipes, ready to march us in to the reception. In we walked, champagne glasses in hand, to that elegant room with the beautiful wallpaper and Queen Anne–style furniture, and a big crackling fire. What a great beginning to a wonderful party! We needed the ceremony to be private, but this was a celebration with about three hundred people.

There were lots of hors d'oeuvres. Our wedding cake was three-tiered, with "Congratulations Molly and Walt" and a little bride and groom on top. But around the bottom tier it said, "Life Begins at 40," and there were forty red candles for my birthday. Everybody sang "Happy Birthday," and I gathered all the children and between us we blew them out. We spent the night in town, stayed at home for Christmas, and then went off by ourselves for a belated honeymoon.

Our wedding celebration was so joyous. Somehow the love that we have for each other kind of blossomed out and touched a lot of other people's lives that day. They all took a little bit of that home with them.

MARRIAGE IN THE CRYSTAL BALL

Marriage is returning to basics. Because most of life will be impersonal and detached, the marriage relationship will become especially important. Young people will weigh the choice of partner by living together and marrying at an older age. Nevertheless, divorce rates will continue to climb. By the year 2000, half of all Americans will have been through one divorce, equally a result of longer life spans as well as changing values. But more than 80 percent of them will remarry.

The "serial" marriage envisioned by Margaret Mead—a new and more appropriate partner for each different stage of adult life—will be ac-cepted. Younger couples and those whose children have left the nest will have an "individual" partnership; "parental" marriage will be the form for those whose primary goal is raising children. The most popular marriage styles will be "companionate" (sharing life together) and "collegial" (sharing interests and work).

Partners will demand quality in the relationship and will work at achieving intimacy, communication, shared recreation time. Having children—there will be fewer—will be postponed until the couple is emotionally and financially ready, and both parents will share in their care.

Up to now, "his" marriage has been better than "her" marriage—and even healthier, studies show. But changes in laws, values, and expectations will make marriage equally fulfilling for both partners.

Achieving privacy will be an ongoing struggle, inside and outside marriage. Since many newlyweds will start out living with in-laws or friends for financial reasons, there will be a need to escape. And so vacations will be fantasies: they will favor exotic places, man-made tropical environments, shared condominiums in otherwise unaffordable places. By the year 2030, when some people may well be living and working in special colonies on the moon, it will be possible for some couples to honeymoon there—and experiment with sex in zero gravity!

As the world has changed, many cultures have evolved into more sophisticated living styles. But throughout human history, men and women have always pursued marriage as a preferred status—and will continue to, even if having several mates in a lifetime becomes the norm. The bride will continue to symbolize that most human constant—life itself—a romantic, exciting adventure.

Acknowledgments

A book such as *The Bride: A Celebration* begins in the heart and mind long before even one word appears on the printed page. For me, this anthology began to take shape on June 13, 1966, when I became Editor-in-Chief of BRIDE'S Magazine. Within just two decades, there have been startling and historic changes—both in attitudes about matrimony and in the behavior patterns of the men and women who wed. And during these same years at Condé Nast—in that very special atmosphere that encourages creative energy and fosters journalistic curiosity—I have been able to develop an overview of marriage and the family that spans the ages and embraces all the many and diverse cultures of humankind. For that opportunity, I take pride and pleasure in expressing my deepest appreciation, especially on the occasion of BRIDE'S Magazine's Fiftieth Anniversary in 1984.

Fervent thanks and applause go out to the many contributors to this book: to Holly Drorbaugh who, as the granddaughter of our founder, Wells Drorbaugh, brought personal as well as professional dedication to this project. Her efforts to research the greatest possible selection of photographs, paintings, objets d'art, and other wedding memorabilia were both tireless and fruitful, and she joins me in thanking both Yvonne Vera and Millie Martini, who aided our search with unfailing enthusiasm.

To Kathy Mullins, who worked side by side with me from outline to finished manuscript, coordinating the researchers' efforts, interviewing our "decade" couples, and weaving her own special magic through each and every page of the text. And to her team: Donna Breining Blass, Sarah T. Boyle, Charlotte Knabel, Anne Mayer, and Antonia van der Meer, who spent one entire summer in libraries and at their typewriters, in order to pay homage to *The Bride*.

Special thanks: to Miriam Arond, whose ability to tame the multitude of pages in this bulky manuscript was unparalleled even in the face of a fast-approaching deadline, and to Andrea Feld, who offered inspiration and nourishment when spirits flagged, as well as generosity of spirit and talent throughout the long process of researching and writing.

To Barbara Tims, who showered us with ideas and sources, most of which are to be found in this volume, and to her staff at British BRIDES Magazine, especially Lillie Davies and Elaine Shaw in the CNP Ltd. Photo Library, for unfailing cooperation in locating and dispatching all those photographs—both popular and obscure—that we requested.

To Diana Edkins, whose guidance in our initial stages was invaluable in getting our pictorial research started. And to Diane Spoto and Cindy Cathcart, for advising us on myriad details as the search unfolded.

To Marcia Vickery, whose words of travel wisdom enliven the honeymoon pages. To Alecia Beldegreen, whose artistic spirit is evident in the cover photograph and who, with Elizabeth Thayer Verney and Ruth MacLeod, shepherded *The Bride* through that last but vital deadline.

To Belle Steinberg, whose search and rescue operation extracted even the most obscure research as we went to press. And to Andrea Furey, who patiently attended to final details.

To our brides of the decades, whose insightful soliloquies called up poignant memories of each era—Bunny Moskowitz, Gunvor Tyler, Eloise

Flowers, Elinor King, Anne Dawson, and Molly Kalin.

To Darlene Geis of Abrams, whose antennae recognized *The Bride* in my future even before I did, and who spirited her along to the finished vision. We are also indebted to Kathie Ness, Barbara Lyons, and Judy Henry, whose editing skills, picture expertise, and design direction have distilled the radiance of the bride on these pages.

And to the many more who supported this project with enthusiasm and who were generous with their time, their archives, and their pictures, I owe a great debt of gratitude: Robert Bachrach of Bachrach Photographers, Jennifer Beeston, Cile Bellefleur Burbidge, Phyllis Caroff, Barbara Norfleet Cohen of Harvard University's Carpenter Center, Mrs. Charles (Page) Dickey, Elizabeth Moxley Falk, Mr. Fang of the Xai Huan Chinese News Agency, Mr. Irving Feld of Ringling Brothers and Barnum & Bailey Circus, Mrs. John (Shirley) Gaither, Jun I. Kanai of The Kyoto Costume Institute, Priscilla and Betsy Kidder of Priscilla of Boston, Shirley Goodman and Harold Koda of The Fashion Institute of Technology, Leonard Lauder, Mrs. Lothian Lynes of The New York Botanical Garden, Mrs. Daniel (Louise) McKeon, Mr. George McManus of Evyan Perfumes, Mrs. Laure Nehgle of The Italian Cultural Institute, Peter and Paul Schaffer and Barbara Perri of A La Vielle Russie, Julie Seymour of James II Galleries, Barbara and Robert Tiffany, and Pat Kerr Tigrett.

And of course, much love and thanks to my family and many friends for their support during my "absence" in the summer of 1983.

B.T.

PHOTO CREDITS

Sources for illustrations are given by page number.

Page 2: Courtesy Leonard Lauder Collection, New York; page 10: Magnum Photos, Inc., photo by Ian Berry; page 12: The Bettmann Archive Inc.; page 13: Culver Pictures, Inc.; page 14: Egyptian Museum, Cairo, photo by Hirmer Verlag, Munich; page 17: Life Magazine © Time, Inc., photo by John Dominis; page 18: From the book *Royal Weddings in Vogue: 1922–1981*, The Condé Nast Publications; page 19: Egyptian Museum, Cairo; page 20: Museum of the American Indian, New York, from a post card of 1895; page 21 above: The Bettmann Archive Inc.; page 22: Whitney Museum of American Art, New York. Gift of Edgar William and Bernice Chrysler Garbisch; page 23: Collection of the artist, Vence; page 24 right: Culver Pictures, Inc.; page 25 above: Courtesy Villery & Bock, New York; page 25 below: Elke Sommer. Published by Edward Weston Graphics, Northridge, CA; page 26: Courtesy Leonard Lauder Collection, New York; page 27 above: Courtesy Pat Kerr; page 27 below: Courtesy *Bride's*, copyright © 1978 The Condé Nast Publications Inc.; page 28: The Bettmann Archive Inc.; page 29: © Copyright 1973 by James Van Der Zee. All rights reserved; page 30: Life Magazine © 1952 Time Inc. By permission of King Features, New York; page 31: FPG International, photo by Underhill; page 32: Life Magazine © Time Inc., photo by Lisa Larsen; page 33: Marisol, Private Collection; page 36: The Bettmann Archive Inc.; page 38: From the book, *Royal Weddings in Vogue: 1922–1981*, The Condé Nast Publications Ltd.; page 39: Watteau, The National Gallery, London; page 40: Museum of Modern Art Stills Archive; page 41: The Bettmann Archive Inc.; page 42 above, left, and right, below: © Winterthur Museum, Courtesy The Henry Francis du Pont Winterthur Museum; page 43: Gustave Klimt, Osterreichische Galerie, Vienna; page 45: Culver Pictures, Inc.; page 46: Henri Rousseau, National Gallery of Art, Washington, DC; page 47 left and right: The Art Institute of Chicago; page 48: Culver Pictures, Inc.; page 50 above: Camera Press, London; page 50 below left: Courtesy Tiffany & Co., New York; below right: The Bettmann Archive Inc.; page 51: Roy Lichtenstein, Private Collection, Italy; page 52: The New-York Historical Society, New York; page 54: FPG International, photo by P. Markow; page 58: Culver Pictures, Inc.; page 59: Magnum Photos, Inc., photo by Wayne Miller; page 60 left: Culver Pictures, Inc.; page 60 right: Cartoon by Clem Scalzitti, Erie, Pennsylvania; page 62: Courtesy Hotel Queen Mary's Wedding Chapel, Long Beach, California; page 63: Courtesy Waldorf Astoria, a Hilton Hotel, New York; page 64: Museum of Modern Art Movie Still Archive; page 67: Grandma Moses, A Country Wedding, Copyright © 1973, Grandma Moses Properties Co., New York; page 68, 69: Courtesy Cartier, Inc.; page 70: Arthur Hughes, Courtesy of Birmingham Museums and Art Gallery, England; page

71: American Antiquarian Society, Worcester, Mass.; page 72: Cartoon by William Walter Haefeli, Chicago; page 74: FPG International, photo by R. Chandler; page 75: Culver Pictures, Inc.; page 76: The Bettmann Archive Inc.; page 78 above: Courtesy Tiffany & Co., New York; page 78 below: Courtesy Steuben Glass, New York; page 79 above and below: Courtesy Tiffany & Co., New York; page 80: Museum of Modern Art Film Stills Archive; page 81: Courtesy Tiffany & Co., photo by Bill Cunningham; page 82: Life Magazine © 1956 Time Inc., photo by Eliott Elisofon; page 84: The Bettmann Archive Inc.; page 85: From the book, *Royal Weddings in Vogue 1922–1981*, The Condé Nast Publications Ltd.; page 88: From *Dolls* by Carl Fox, Harry N. Abrams, Inc., Publisher, photo by Herman Landshoff; page 89: The Brooklyn Museum, Gift of Mrs. Russell Davenport; page 90: © American Museum of Natural History; page 91: Israel Museum, Jerusalem, photo by Nahum Slapak; page 92: FPG International; page 93: From *Leslie's Sunday Magazine*, Nov. 1880, Culver Pictures, Inc.; page 94: Private Archive; page 95: Courtesy *Bride's*, copyright © The Condé Nast Publications Inc. 1983; page 96; Courtesy Harry S. Truman Library, Independence, MO; page 97: From the book, *Royal Weddings in Vogue 1922–1981*, The Condé Nast Publications Ltd.; page 99: Courtesy *Bride's*, Copyright © The Condé Nast Publications Inc. 1982; page 100 above: HNA Archives; page 100 below: Lord West Formal Wear and Accessories, New York; page 101: FPG International; page 103: Culver Pictures, Inc.; page 105: The Collections of The Library of Congress; page 106: FPG International; page 107: Cara Goldberg Mark, illustrator; page 108: Copyright © James Van Der Zee, 1981, All rights reserved; page 109: FPG International; page 110 left: FPG International, photo by Paul de Paola; page 110 right: From the book, *Bride's Complete Guide to Planning Your Wedding*, The Condé Nast Publications Ltd., 1983; page 111: Courtesy Pat Kerr; page 112: Museum of Modern Art Film Stills Archive; page 113: The Mansell Collection; page 114: FPG International, photo by Paul C. Pet; page 115: Courtesy Shirley and John Gaither, photo by Richard L. Bowditch III; page 117, above, left, and right: FPG International; page 118: Cake created by Cile Bellefleur Burbidge; page 120: Camera Press, Ltd., London; page 122 left: FPG International; page 122 right: Life Magazine © 1945 Time Inc., photo by Frank Scherschel; page 123: Museum of Modern Art Film Stills Archive; page 124: © Robert Balzer, from *Wines of California*, Harry N. Abrams, Inc. Publisher; page 125: Magnum Photos, Inc., © 1969, photo by Wayne Miller; page 126: Magnum Photos, Inc., photo by Richard Klavar; page 127 left: Private Archive; page 127 right: FPG International, photo by P. Dallas; page 128: From *Bride's Complete Guide to Planning Your Wedding* © The Condé Nast Publications Ltd.; page 129: FPG In-

ACKNOWLEDGMENT OF PERMISSIONS